First World War
and Army of Occupation
War Diary
France, Belgium and Germany

56 DIVISION
Divisional Troops
513 Field Company Royal Engineers
1 February 1915 - 30 April 1919

WO95/2942/3

The Naval & Military Press Ltd
www.nmarchive.com
Published in association with The National Archives

Published by

The Naval & Military Press Ltd

Unit 10 Ridgewood Industrial Park,

Uckfield, East Sussex,

TN22 5QE England

Tel: +44 (0) 1825 749494

www.naval-military-press.com

www.nmarchive.com

This diary has been reprinted in facsimile from the original. Any imperfections are inevitably reproduced and the quality may fall short of modern type and cartographic standards.

Contents

Document type	Place/Title	Date From	Date To
Heading	WO95/2942/3		
Heading	513th Field Coy R.E. Feb 1916-Apr 1919.		
Heading	2/2 London Fd Coy R.E. Vol I		
Heading	2/2 London Fd Coy RE Feb Vol II		
Heading	2/2 London Fd Coy RE Vol 2		
War Diary	Needham Market	01/02/1915	21/02/1915
War Diary	Havre	22/02/1915	22/02/1915
War Diary	Hocquincourt	23/02/1915	28/02/1915
War Diary	Bouchon	01/03/1916	01/03/1916
War Diary	Mouflers	02/03/1916	14/03/1916
War Diary	Sars Lez Bois	15/03/1916	30/04/1916
War Diary	Duisans	01/05/1916	04/05/1916
War Diary	Manin	05/05/1916	05/05/1916
War Diary	Henu	06/05/1916	08/05/1916
War Diary	Hebuterne	09/05/1916	25/06/1916
War Diary	S Amand	26/06/1916	30/06/1916
War Diary	Sailly. Au. Bois.	01/07/1916	02/07/1916
War Diary	Souastre	03/07/1916	25/07/1916
War Diary	Bienvillers	26/07/1916	31/07/1916
Heading	56th Divisional Engineers 2/2nd London Field Company R.E. August 1916.		
War Diary	Bienvillers	01/08/1916	18/08/1916
War Diary	Ivergny	19/08/1916	22/08/1916
War Diary	Benatre	23/08/1916	23/08/1916
War Diary	Neuf Moulin	24/08/1916	31/08/1916
Miscellaneous	Progress Report	01/08/1916	01/08/1916
Miscellaneous	Progress Report	02/08/1916	02/08/1916
Miscellaneous	Progress Report	03/08/1916	03/08/1916
Miscellaneous	Progress Report	04/08/1916	04/08/1916
Miscellaneous	Progress Report		
Miscellaneous	Progress Report	05/08/1916	05/08/1916
Miscellaneous	Progress Report	06/08/1916	06/08/1916
Miscellaneous	Progress Report	07/08/1916	07/08/1916
Miscellaneous	Progress Report	08/08/1916	08/08/1916
Miscellaneous	Progress Report		
Miscellaneous	Progress Report	09/08/1916	09/08/1916
Miscellaneous	Progress Report		
Miscellaneous	Progress Report	11/08/1916	11/08/1916
Miscellaneous	Progress Report	12/08/1916	12/08/1916
Miscellaneous	Progress Report	13/08/1916	13/08/1916
Miscellaneous	Progress Report	14/08/1916	14/08/1916
Miscellaneous	Progress Report	15/08/1916	15/08/1916
Miscellaneous	Progress Report		
Miscellaneous	Progress Report	17/08/1916	17/08/1916
Heading	56th Divisional Engineers 2/2nd London Field Company R.E. September 1916.		
War Diary	Neuf Moulin	01/09/1916	03/09/1916
War Diary	Corbie	04/09/1916	04/09/1916
War Diary	Happy Valley Camp	05/09/1916	05/09/1916
War Diary	Bronfoy Farm	06/09/1916	12/09/1916

War Diary	Bronfoy Farm Camp	13/09/1916	14/09/1916
War Diary	Battle H Qs	15/09/1916	27/09/1916
War Diary	Meaulte	28/09/1916	30/09/1916
War Diary	Bernafay Wood	09/10/1916	09/10/1916
War Diary	Citadel	10/10/1916	10/10/1916
War Diary	Yseaux	11/10/1916	20/10/1916
War Diary	Erondelle	21/10/1916	23/10/1916
War Diary	Calonne	24/10/1916	27/10/1916
War Diary	8 Maisons	28/10/1916	31/10/1916
War Diary	Huit Maisons	01/11/1916	20/12/1916
War Diary	Laventie	21/12/1916	02/02/1917
War Diary	Huit Maisons	03/02/1917	09/03/1917
War Diary	La Gorgue	09/03/1917	09/03/1917
War Diary	Robecq	10/03/1917	10/03/1917
War Diary	Valhoun	11/03/1917	11/03/1917
War Diary	Oppy	12/03/1917	13/03/1917
War Diary	Simencourt	14/03/1917	14/03/1917
War Diary	Achicourt	15/03/1917	19/04/1917
War Diary	Souastre	20/04/1917	23/04/1917
War Diary	Wanquetin	24/04/1917	25/04/1917
War Diary	Wanquetin Berneville	26/04/1917	26/04/1917
War Diary	Berneville	27/04/1917	27/04/1917
War Diary	Arras	28/04/1917	30/04/1917
Operation(al) Order(s)	56th Divisional Engineers Order No. 95.	27/04/1917	27/04/1917
War Diary	Arras	01/05/1917	19/05/1917
War Diary	Duisans	20/05/1917	23/05/1917
War Diary	Gouves	24/05/1917	31/05/1917
War Diary	Arras-Tilloy	01/06/1917	28/06/1917
War Diary	Tilloy	29/06/1917	30/06/1917
Miscellaneous	Messages And Signals.		
Operation(al) Order(s)	56th Divisional Engineers Order No. 104.	27/06/1917	27/06/1917
War Diary	Tilloy & Grand Rullecourt	01/07/1917	02/07/1917
War Diary	Gouy & Grand Rullecourt	03/07/1917	03/07/1917
War Diary	Sombrin	04/07/1917	21/07/1917
War Diary	Bouquemaison	22/07/1917	22/07/1917
War Diary	Hallines	23/07/1917	23/07/1917
War Diary	Westrove	24/07/1917	04/08/1917
War Diary	Nordpreene	05/08/1917	05/08/1917
War Diary	Wippenhoek	06/08/1917	10/08/1917
War Diary	Chateau Segard	11/08/1917	17/08/1917
War Diary	Wippenhoek	18/08/1917	24/08/1917
War Diary	Westrove	24/08/1917	29/08/1917
War Diary	Wizernes	30/08/1917	30/08/1917
War Diary	Bapaume Bancourt Road Camp	31/08/1917	31/08/1917
Operation(al) Order(s)	169th Infantry Brigade Order No. 107.	04/08/1917	04/08/1917
Miscellaneous	March Table		
Operation(al) Order(s)	56th Divisional Engineers Order No. 108.	11/08/1917	11/08/1917
Operation(al) Order(s)	56th Divisional Engineers Order No. 110	12/08/1917	12/08/1917
Operation(al) Order(s)	56th Divisional Engineers Order No. 116	17/08/1917	17/08/1917
Miscellaneous	March Table		
Operation(al) Order(s)	56th Divisional Engineers Order No. 117	22/08/1917	22/08/1917
Miscellaneous	March Table		
War Diary	Bapaume-Bancourt Camp	01/09/1917	04/09/1917
War Diary	Lebucquiere	05/09/1917	02/12/1917
War Diary	Dainville	03/12/1917	04/12/1917
War Diary	Maroeuil	05/12/1917	06/12/1917

War Diary	Ecurie	07/12/1917	19/12/1917
War Diary	St Catherine Arras	20/12/1917	31/01/1918
War Diary	Aubrey Camp St Catharine	01/02/1918	08/02/1918
War Diary	Chantecler H.1d 1.7	09/02/1918	28/02/1918
Heading	War Diary 513th Field Company R.E. March 1918		
War Diary	Arras H 1d1.7.	01/03/1918	12/03/1918
War Diary	Arras Chantecler H1.d.1.7.	13/03/1918	30/03/1918
War Diary	Anzin G.7.b.5.9	31/03/1918	31/03/1918
Heading	56th Divisional Engineers 513rd Field Company R.E. April 1918		
War Diary	Anzin-St-Aubin G.7.b.4.9.	01/04/1918	05/04/1918
War Diary	Estree-Cauchie W.2.a.	06/04/1918	07/04/1918
War Diary	Agnes-Les-Duissans K.12.b.2.7.	08/04/1918	08/04/1918
War Diary	Wagnonlieu L.22.c.1.8.	09/04/1918	09/04/1918
War Diary	Ronville Caves G.34.b.56.48.	10/04/1918	28/04/1918
War Diary	Arras G.27.b.15.90.	29/04/1918	14/07/1918
War Diary	Wagnonlieu Sheet 51c L21d9.6.	15/04/1918	15/04/1918
War Diary	Beugin P.7a5.5 Sheet No 44b	15/07/1918	17/07/1918
War Diary	Bajus O22b1.1 Sheet 44b	18/07/1918	30/07/1918
War Diary	Cambligneul W.14.d.	31/07/1918	01/08/1918
War Diary	Arras G.27.b.15.90.	02/08/1918	17/08/1918
War Diary	Denier I.19.a.8.0.	18/08/1918	19/08/1918
War Diary	Arras	20/08/1918	20/08/1918
War Diary	Fosseux	21/08/1918	21/08/1918
War Diary	Saulty V.2.a	22/08/1918	23/08/1918
War Diary	Bailleulval W.3.b.	24/08/1918	24/08/1918
War Diary	Boiseux-Au-Mont S.9.d.9.3.	25/08/1918	07/09/1918
War Diary	O8d4.2	07/09/1918	07/09/1918
War Diary	Sheet 51b SW O8d4.2 Remy. O 18c.5.5	08/09/1918	13/09/1918
War Diary	Remy Sheet 51b SW O18.c.5.5	14/09/1918	19/09/1918
War Diary	Sheet 51b SE P.32d4.5.	20/09/1918	27/09/1918
War Diary	Baralle W.8.c.2.1.	28/09/1918	29/09/1918
War Diary	Rumacourt Q.20.c.7.2.	29/09/1918	15/10/1918
War Diary	Maroeuil	16/10/1918	31/10/1918
War Diary	Pave	01/11/1918	02/11/1918
War Diary	Thiant	03/11/1918	04/11/1918
War Diary	Saultain	05/11/1918	05/11/1918
War Diary	Sebourg Sheet 51 A20.d.0.9.	06/11/1918	07/11/1918
War Diary	Autreppe B19c7.7 Sheet 51.	08/11/1918	10/11/1918
War Diary	Fayt Le Franc B18a.5.4	11/11/1918	26/11/1918
War Diary	Bougnies Sheet 45 W.19a1.5	27/11/1918	29/11/1918
War Diary	Asquillies Sheet 45 W.8.c.8.8.	30/11/1918	31/01/1919
War Diary	Asquillies Map Ref Belgium And Part Of France Sheet 45 Ed3 1:40,000 W.8.c.8.8.	01/02/1919	11/02/1919
War Diary	Asquillies (Sheet 4.5.) W.8.c.8.8.	12/02/1919	16/03/1919
War Diary	Asquilles	17/03/1919	19/03/1919
War Diary	Jemappes	20/03/1919	31/03/1919
War Diary	Jemappes Mons	01/04/1919	30/04/1919

56TH DIVISION

513TH FIELD COY R.E.

FEB 1916 - APR 1919.

56

2/2 London Fd Coy
R.E.

Vol I

56 D

2

56

2/2 London Fd Coy
R E

Feb

Vol II

56

2/2 London Fd Coy
R E

Vol 2

Secret.

Instructions regarding War Diaries and Intelligence Summaries are contained in F. S. Regs., Part II. and the Staff Manual respectively. Title pages will be prepared in manuscript.

WAR DIARY

~~or~~

~~INTELLIGENCE SUMMARY.~~

(Erase heading not required.)

Army Form C. 2118.

2/2nd London Field Coy RE.

Place	Date	Hour	Summary of Events and Information	Remarks and references to Appendices
NEEDHAM MARKET	1/2/15 to 13/2/15		Nil.	G.T.K
	14/2/15		Orders received to embark for overseas on Monday 21/2/15	G.T.K
	15/2/15 to 20/2/15		Nil	G.T.K
	21/2/15	6.50 am	Unit entrained less 2 sections + half HQ for Southampton	
		9.30	2 sections + ½ HQ entrained for Southampton.	
HAVRE	22/2/15	2. am	Arrived Havre & proceeded No 5 Dock Rest Camp	G.T.K
HOCQUINCOURT	23/2/15	5.20 pm	Left Rest Camp & entrained at No 1 Point	
"	24/2/15	8.15 am	Arrived ~~Pont~~ REMY Station. Detrained & proceeded into Billets at HOCQUINCOURT	G.T.K
	25/2/15 to 26/2/15		Nil	G.T.K
	27/2/15	10 am	Left HOCQUINCOURT & proceeded by road with 168 Bde to BOUCHON.	G.T.K
	28/2/15 29/2/15		At BOUCHON	G.T.K

G. T. Kingsford
MAJOR R.E., T.
O.C., 2nd/2nd LONDON FIELD CO.

Secret

Instructions regarding War Diaries and Intelligence Summaries are contained in F. S. Regs., Part II. and the Staff Manual respectively. Title pages will be prepared in manuscript.

WAR DIARY
or
~~INTELLIGENCE SUMMARY.~~
(Erase heading not required.)

Army Form C. 2118.

2/2nd London Field Coy RE.

Place	Date	Hour	Summary of Events and Information	Remarks and references to Appendices
BOUCHON	1 3/16	-	Nil	G.T.K
MOUFLERS	2 3/16	2.30pm	Left billets at BOUCHON & proceeded by road to Billets at MOUFLERS	G.T.K
MOUFLERS	3 3/16 to 11 3/16		Nil	G.T.K
MOUFLERS	12 3/16	8 am	Left MOUFLERS with 168 Brigade & proceeded by Road to BRETEL	G.T.K
"	13 3/16 14 3/16		Nil	G.T.K
SARS LEZ BOIS	15 3/16	8.30am	Left BRETEL & proceeded by Road to SARS LEZ BOIS	G.T.K
	16 3/16		Nil	G.T.K
	17 3/16		No 3 Section (Lieut R.O. Beit RE) detached for work at Div. Hd Qrs LE CAUROY	G.T.K
	18 3/16 to 26 3/16		Nil	
	27 3/16		Nos 1 & 2 Sections (Lt J.E. Villa & 2Lt W.A.R. Bourne) under command of Capt A.O. Laird detached to take over from 2/1st London Field Coy RE at HONVAL	G.T.K
	28 3/16 to 31 3/16		Nil	G.T.K

G.T. Kingsford
Major RE

1577 Wt. W10791/1773 500,000 1/15 D. D. & L. A.D.S.S./Forms/C. 2118.

Secret

Instructions regarding War Diaries and Intelligence Summaries are contained in F. S. Regs., Part II. and the Staff Manual respectively. Title pages will be prepared in manuscript.

WAR DIARY
or
~~INTELLIGENCE SUMMARY.~~
(Erase heading not required.)

Army Form C. 2118.

2/2nd London Field Co. R.E.

Place	Date	Hour	Summary of Events and Information	Remarks and references to Appendices
SARS LEZ BOIS	1 4/16 to 11 4/16		Nil	G.T.K
	11 4/16		Reinforcement of 4 sappers received from Base	G.T.K
	12 4/16		Nos 1 & 2 sections (Lt Villa & 2/Lt Bourne) under command of Capt Laird left HONVAL & proceeded to ARRAS for attachment to 61 & 62 Fd Coys respectively	G.T.K
	13 4/16		~~[illegible]~~ No 3 Section (Lt Beit) rejoined unit from detachment at LE CADROY. HQ & Nos 3 & 4 sections (Lt Beit & 2Lt Dain) by road to DUISANS to take over work of 2/1st London Fd Co RE on Corps line	G.T.K
	16 4/16		1 OR evacuated to C.C. Station	G.T.K
	17 4/16 to 22 4/16		Nil	G.T.K
	23 4/16		1 OR evacuated to C.C. station	
	24 4/16 to 30 4/16		Nil	G.T.K

G T Ringsford Maj RE
OC 2/2nd London Fd Co RE

1577 Wt. W10791/1773 500,000 1/15 D. D. & L. A.D.S.S./Forms/C. 2118.

56

Instructions regarding War Diaries and Intelligence Summaries are contained in F. S. Regs., Part II. and the Staff Manual respectively. Title pages will be prepared in manuscript.

WAR DIARY
or
~~INTELLIGENCE SUMMARY.~~
(Erase heading not required.)

Army Form C. 2118.

2/2nd LONDON FIELD COY RE

Vol 3

Place	Date	Hour	Summary of Events and Information	Remarks and references to Appendices
DUISANS	1/5/16		Mounted portions of Nos 1 & 2 sections returned to the Company.	G.T.K.
	2/5/16			
	3/5/16		Nil	G.T.K.
	4/5/16		Orders received for Company to return to 56th Divn. Work on Corps line handed over to 235 A.T. Coy RE & works on ARRAS front to 61st 62nd & 89th Fd Coys RE. 8 Other ranks proceeded to Base on reduction of Establishment	G.T.K.
MANIN	5/5/16	4.30am	Company moved from DUISANS (2 sections i/c Capt LAIRD having rejoined from ARRAS) to MANIN arriving 8.30 am & occupied billets	G.T.K.
HÉNU	6/5/16	3 pm	Company moved with 168th Brigade to billets in HÉNU arriving 9 pm & joining the VII Corps with the remainder of 56 Divn	G.T.K.
	7/5/16		2 O.R. joined Company from Base	G.T.K.
	8/5/16		1 O.R. joined Company from Base	G.T.K.
HEBUTERNE	9/5/16	7 pm	Company less No 1 section (Lt Villa) & No 2 section (2/Lt Bourne) left HÉNU & proceeded to HEBUTERNE. HQ (less O.C. Captain CAMS & P.S.) proceeding thence to billets in BAYENCOURT.	G.T.K.
	10/5/16		Took over dug'outs in HEBUTERNE & prepared them for occupation	G.T.K.

1577 Wt. W10791/1773 500,000 1/15 D. D. & L. A.D.S.S./Forms/C. 2118.

Instructions regarding War Diaries and Intelligence Summaries are contained in F. S. Regs., Part II. and the Staff Manual respectively. Title pages will be prepared in manuscript.

WAR DIARY
or
~~INTELLIGENCE SUMMARY.~~
(Erase heading not required.)

Army Form C. 2118.

2/2nd London 7th Coy RE

Place	Date	Hour	Summary of Events and Information	Remarks and references to Appendices
HEBUTERNE	11/5/16		Took over Right sector of 56 Div front from 2/1st London 7th Coy RE	GTK.
"	12/5/16		Nil	GTK
	13/5/16		1 OR to Base depot	
	14/5/16		Nil	GTK
	15/5/16		Nil.	GTK
	16/5/16		2 other ranks killed during bombardment of front line trenches at 12.30 am. & 2 other ranks wounded	
			1 other rank to casualty clearing stat in sick	GTK
	17/5/16		Nil.	GTK
	18/5/16		Nil	GTK
	19/5/16		Nil	GTK
	20/5/16		Nil	GTK
	21/5/16		1 OR rejoined from C.C.S. Capt A O Laird & 1 OR proceeded on leave.	GTK
	22/5/16		Nil	
	23/5/16		Nil	
	24/5/16		Nil	

Instructions regarding War Diaries and Intelligence Summaries are contained in F. S. Regs., Part II. and the Staff Manual respectively. Title Pages will be prepared in manuscript.

WAR DIARY
or
INTELLIGENCE SUMMARY
(Erase heading not required.)

Army Form C. 2118

Place	Date	Hour	Summary of Events and Information	Remarks and references to Appendices
HEBUTERNE	25/5/16		Nil	GTK
	26/5/16		Nil	GTK
	27/5/16		Nil	GTK
	28/5		Nil	GTK.
	29/5		1 OR to C.C.S. – Lt Villa & 2 OR proceeded on leave.	GTK
	30/5		1 O.R. wounded to C.C.S	GTK
	31/5		1 OR killed. 1 OR returned from leave.	GTK
	1/6			

G. T. Kingsford
Major RE
OC 2/2nd London Fd Co RE

Instructions regarding War Diaries and Intelligence Summaries are contained in F. S. Regs., Part II. and the Staff Manual respectively. Title Pages will be prepared in manuscript.

WAR DIARY
or
INTELLIGENCE SUMMARY
(Erase heading not required.)

Army Form C. 2118

2/2nd London Field Coy RE

Vol 4

Place	Date	Hour	Summary of Events and Information	Remarks and references to Appendices
HEBUTERNE	1/6/16		Nil	
	2/6/16		Capt A O Laird reported for duty from leave	
	3/6/16		Nil	
	4/6/16		No 4 Section (2Lt C H R DAIN) proceeded to billet in HENU to work under direct orders of C.R.E. 56th Divn + No 2 section (2Lt W.A.R. BOURNE) left HENU + reported for duty in HEBUTERNE	
	5/6/16		Major G.T. Kingsford + 2 OR proceeded on leave - 1 O.R. evacuated to C.C.S. (Sick).	A.O.L
	6/6/16		Nil	A.O.L
	7/6/16		4 O.R from Base.	A.O.L
	8/6/16		Lt Beit and 1 O.R. proceeded to WARLUS to attend forcing jack demonstration. Lt J.E Villa reported for duty from leave - 1 O.R. returned from leave - 1 O.R from Base	A.O.L
	9/6/16		nil.	
	10/6/16		nil.	
	11/6/16		1 O.R. proceeded on leave	A.O.L
	12/6/16		2 O.R to C.C.S.	A.O.L
	13/6		1 O.R to C.C.S.	G.T.K
	14/6		1 O.R joined from Base	G.T.K
	15/6		Nil	G.T.K
	16/6		2 O.R returned from leave	G.T.K
	17/6		Nil	G.T.K
	18/6		Major Kingsford returned from leave. 1 O.R killed No 1 Section left Hebuterne + proceeded to GRENAS for attachment to 168 Bde	G.T.K

1875 Wt. W593/826 1,000,000 4/15 J.B.C. & A. A.D.S.S./Forms/C. 2118.

Instructions regarding War Diaries and Intelligence Summaries are contained in F. S. Regs., Part II. and the Staff Manual respectively. Title Pages will be prepared in manuscript.

WAR DIARY
or
INTELLIGENCE SUMMARY
(Erase heading not required.)

Army Form C. 2118

Place	Date	Hour	Summary of Events and Information	Remarks and references to Appendices
HEBOTERNE	19/6		No 3 Sect left HEBUTERNE & proceeded to St AMAND.	GTK
	20/6		Nil	GTK
	21/6		Nil	GTK
	22/6		Nil	GTK
	23/6	10am	Capt Laing left HEBOTERNE & proceeded to St AMAND	GTK
	24/6		Nil	GTK
	25/6		One OR proceeded on leave	GTK
St AMAND.	26/6	6am	HQ & No 2 section left HEBOTERNE & proceeded to St AMAND	GTK
	27/6		Nil	GTK
	28/6		Two O.R evacuated to C.C.S. 5 O.R. joined from Base.	GTK
	29/6		Nil	GTK
	30/6	12 midnight	HQ & Nos 2 & 3 sections left StAMAND & proceeded into Div' Reserve at SAILLY AU BOIS	GTK

G. T. Dangerfield
MAJOR R.E., T.,
O.C., 2nd/2nd LONDON FIELD CO.

1875 Wt. W593/826 1,000,000 4/15 J.B.C. & A. A.D.S.S./Forms/C. 2118.

SECRET.

Instructions regarding War Diaries and Intelligence Summaries are contained in F. S. Regs., Part II. and the Staff Manual respectively. Title Pages will be prepared in manuscript.

WAR DIARY
or
INTELLIGENCE SUMMARY
(Erase heading not required.)

56 Divn

Army Form C. 2118

2/2nd London Field Coy R.E.

Vol 5

Place	Date	Hour	Summary of Events and Information	Remarks and references to Appendices
SAILLY-AU-BOIS	1/7/16		No 1 Section (Lt Villa RE) attached to London Scottish Battn & advanced with their attack South of Gommecourt reaching their objective but were forced to retire all ammunition having been expended & their flanks being exposed. 1 O.R. killed 7 OR Missing & 8 OR wounded. 1. OR killed & Capt A O Laird RE wounded in attempting to disarm a soldier amok. No 4 section (Lt Dain RE) left HENU & reported for duty at SAILLY AU BOIS	G.T.K
	2/7/16		Lt Villa RE & No 1 Section proceeded to HENU. Remainder of Company proceeded to ~~Hu~~ billets in SOUASTRE.	[illegible]
SOUASTRE	3/7/16		Nos 3 & 4 Sections (Lt Beit & Dain RE) proceeded to FONQUEVILLERS for work in sector occupied by 168 Bde	G.T.K
	4/7/16		No 1 Section rejoined Company at SOUASTRE from HENU	G.T.K
	5/7/16		Nil	[illegible]
	6/7/16		23 OR joined Company from Base	G.T.K.
	7/7/16		Nil	[illegible]
	8/7/16		Nil	[illegible]
	9/7/16		3 OR's reported evacuated on 26, 28 & 29 June	[illegible]
	10/7/16		1 OR wounded by grenade in FONQUEVILLERS & evacuated	G.T.K
	11/7/16		Nil	G.T.K
	12/7/16		Nil	G.T.K

1875 Wt. W593/826 1,000,000 4/15 J.B.C. & A. A.D.S.S./Forms/C. 2118.

SECRET.

Instructions regarding War Diaries and Intelligence Summaries are contained in F. S. Regs., Part II. and the Staff Manual respectively. Title Pages will be prepared in manuscript.

WAR DIARY
or
INTELLIGENCE SUMMARY
(Erase heading not required.)

Army Form C. 2118

Place	Date	Hour	Summary of Events and Information	Remarks and references to Appendices
SOUASTRE	13/7/16		1 OR reported evacuated on 8th inst.	GJK
	14/7/16		Capt F.R. Lewin & 2/Lt H.G. Pinnock joined from base	GJK
	15/7/16		Nil	GJK
	16/7/16		No 2 Section (Lt Bonner) relieved No 3 section (Lt Best) in FONQUEVILLERS & No 3 section returned to SOUASTRE.	
			6 OR attached to 2nd London Battn for explosive duties in connection with raid on German front line.	
			One OR. wounded.	[illegible]
			Capt. O.A. LAIRD evacuated on 4th inst.	
	17.7.16		Nil.	[illegible]
	18.7.16		M/G gun emplacements begun for P.P.	[illegible]
	19.7.16		SOUASTRE baths completed.	[illegible]
	20.7.16		Y.M.C.A. hut (SOUASTRE) completed.	
			Huts dismantled at GAUDIEMPRE.	[illegible]
	21.7.16		Repair work begun on O.P. for BARKHOW.	[illegible]
			BIENVILLERS baths begun.	
			Deep dug-out begun for HARGUN. (BIENVILLERS.)	
	22.7.16		Deep dug-outs begun for SOART, BARKHOW, R.A.M.C., R.E. (all at BIENVILLERS).	
			Lieut. E.G. Small, Lieut. T.P.B. Cliff, Lieut. M. Macfarlane reported from base.	[illegible]

1875 Wt. W593/826 1,000,000 4/15 J.B.C. & A. A.D.S.S./Forms/C. 2118.

SECRET.

Instructions regarding War Diaries and Intelligence Summaries are contained in F. S. Regs., Part II. and the Staff Manual respectively. Title Pages will be prepared in manuscript.

WAR DIARY
or
INTELLIGENCE SUMMARY
(Erase heading not required.)

Army Form C. 2118

2/2. LONDON FIELD Coy. R.E.(T).

Place	Date	Hour	Summary of Events and Information	Remarks and references to Appendices
SOUASTRE	23/7/16.		No 1 Section (Front-Villa) relieved No 4 section (Front-Lanes) at FONQUEVILLERS. No 4 Section returned to SOUASTRE.	[initials]
	24/7/16.		Nil.	[initials]
	25/7/16.		1. O.R. evacuated. Coy. H.Q. moved to BIENVILLERS.	[initials]
BIENVILLERS.	26/7/16		Coy. H.Q. dugout begun CRAWLBOYS LANE. Repair of wells at ST. AMAND.	[initials]
"	27/7/16		2. O.R. joined from base. Machine gun dugout & emplacement begun for COOT. O.P. repairs for Southern Group Survey Corps. Repairs to pump at baths SOUASTRE.	[initials]
"	28/7/16		2 O.R. evacuated. Repairs to wells Valley Huts, SOUASTRE and at ST. AMAND	[initials]
"	29/7/16		Erecting huts GAUDIEMPRE (Town Major) No 3 Section (Front-Bert) removed to BIENVILLERS.	[initials]
"	30/7/16		Baths at BIENVILLERS ready for use (not completed).	[initials]
"	31/7/16.		Specimen fire-bay begun 2.54. Coy. H.Q. dugout ROBINSON LANE begun.	[initials]

G. T. Mungford[?]
Major R.E.

1875 Wt. W593/826 1,000,000 4/15 J.B.C. & A. A.D.S.S./Forms/C. 2118.

56th Divisional Engineers

2/2nd LONDON FIELD COMPANY R. E.

AUGUST 1 9 1 6 ::

Secret

WAR DIARY
or
~~INTELLIGENCE~~ SUMMARY

(Erase heading not required.)

Army Form C. 2118

Instructions regarding War Diaries and Intelligence Summaries are contained in F. S. Regs., Part II. and the Staff Manual respectively. Title Pages will be prepared in manuscript.

2/2nd London F^d Coy R.E.

Vol 6

Place	Date	Hour	Summary of Events and Information	Remarks and references to Appendices
~~Beinvillers~~ BIENVILLERS	Aug 1st		NIL	G.T.K.
	2nd		NIL	T.T.K.
	3rd		One O.R. joined Unit from Base	G.T.K.
	4th		Capt F.R. Unsworn left for FONQUEVILLERS to take charge of detachment	G.T.K.
	5th		NIL	G.T.K.
	6th		NIL	G.T.K.
	7th		No 1 Section left FONQUEVILLERS for BEINVILLERS in command of 2/Lt PINNOCK	
	"		No 2 " " FONQUEVILLERS for ~~[struck out]~~ SOUASTRE " " 2/Lt BOURNE 2/Lt MACFARLANE	
	"		No 3 " " BEINVILLERS for FONQUEVILLERS " " 2/Lt SMAIL	T.T.K.
	"		No 4 " " SOUASTRE for FONQUEVILLERS " " 2/Lt DAIN 2/Lt CLIFF	
	8th		One O.R. evacuated to C.C.S.	T.T.K.
	9th		~~[struck out]~~ One O.R. Died in Hospital of 2/2nd London Field Amb at GAUDIEMPRE One other Rank joined from BASE	G.T.K.
	10th		NIL	T.T.K.
	11th		NIL	T.T.K.
	12th		NIL	T.T.K.
	13th		NIL	G.T.K.
				G.T.K.

1875 Wt. W593/826 1,000,000 4/15 J.B.C. & A. A.D.S.S./Forms/C. 2118.

Instructions regarding War Diaries and Intelligence Summaries are contained in F. S. Regs., Part II. and the Staff Manual respectively. Title Pages will be prepared in manuscript.

WAR DIARY
or
~~INTELLIGENCE SUMMARY~~
(Erase heading not required.)

Army Form C. 2118

2/2nd London Fd Co RE

Place	Date	Hour	Summary of Events and Information	Remarks and references to Appendices
BIENVILLERS	14th		1 O.R. Returned home to England under age	G.T.K.
	15th		NIL	G.T.K.
	16th		NIL	
	17th		No. 1 Section (+ HQ) moved from BIENVILLERS to ST AMAND } Major G.T. KINGSFORD, 2/Lt PINNOCK HQ, Lt BEIT R.O.	G.T.K.
	"		No 2 Section moved from SOUASTRE to ST AMAND } 2/Lt BOURNE W.A., 2/Lt MACFARLANE	
	"		No 3 Section moved from FONQUEVILLERS to ST AMAND } CAPT. UNWIN + Lt VILLA, 2/Lt DAIN, 2/Lt CLIFF	
	"		No 4 Section moved from " to "	
	"		9 O.R. joined from BASE 1 O.R. to C.C.S.	G.T.K.
	18th		The Company under Command of Major G.T. KINGSFORD moved from ST AMAND to IVERGNY 1 O.R. to C.C.S.	G.T.K.
IVERGNY	19th		NIL	G.T.K.
"	20th		NIL	G.T.K.
"	21st		1 O.R. returned from C.C.S. 2 O.R. returned from CAMP COMMANDANT VII CORPS. 1 O.R. to C.C.S.	G.T.K.
	22nd		The Company under Command of Major G.T. Kingsford moved from IVERGNY to BENATRE with 169th Bde	
BENATRE	23rd		The Company under Command of Major G.T. KINGSFORD moved from BENATRE to NEUF-MOULIN 2/Lt Jeudie (?) rejoined unit from detachment at FONQUEVILLERS.	G.T.K.
NEUF MOULIN	24th		4 Officers + 84 O.R. from 2nd London Regiment, Q.W.R., Q.V.R. + L.R.B. joined Company to take course of training	G.T.K.

1875 Wt. W593/826 1,000,000 4/15 J.B.C. & A. A.D.S.S./Forms/C. 2118.

Army Form C. 2118

WAR DIARY
or
~~INTELLIGENCE SUMMARY~~
(Erase heading not required.)

Instructions regarding War Diaries and Intelligence Summaries are contained in F. S. Regs., Part II. and the Staff Manual respectively. Title Pages will be prepared in manuscript.

2/2nd London Fd Co RE

Place	Date	Hour	Summary of Events and Information	Remarks and references to Appendices
NEUF MOULIN	25/8/16		NIL	G.T.K
	26/8/16		[redacted] 2 O.R. to C.C.S. 1 O.R. returned from C.C.S.	G.T.K
	27/8/16		NIL	G.T.K
	28/8/16		NIL	G.T.K
	29/8/16		3 O.R. to BASE evacuated	G.T.K
	30/8/16		1 O.R. to BASE for Course of duty as L Training Instructor	G.T.K
	31/8/16		Nil	G.T.K

G.T. [illegible] Maj: RE

1875 Wt. W593/826 1,000,000 4/15 J.B.C. & A. A.D.S.S./Forms/C. 2118.

PROGRESS REPORT FOR 24 HOURS TO 2 p.m. 1/8/16 1916.

REFERENCE TO MAP SHEET 57d.S.E. 1/10000

NUMBER EMPLOYED		NATURE OF WORK	AT.		TOTAL NUMBER OF YARDS COMPLETED	REMAINING TO BE DONE	REMARKS.
R.E.	INFANTRY		FROM	TO.			
18	75	Regent St C.T. drainage & repair	E21 b 15.15	E 22 c 6 4 Bazelle Rd.	900		3 Shifts round clock. on all jobs.
			E 22 c 6 4	E 22 d 05 15 Green St			100 yds cleared. One shift interfered with by shelling. Water being pumped & mud cleared
			E 22 d 05.15	E 22 d 3 3 Robinson Lane.			
6	45	Roberts Avenue repair for winter	E 21 d 2.5				About 50' trench boards cleared & trench cleared. As sappers are required for III Army listening OP's & Int[?] are needed to measure parties on other jobs this is being postp[oned]
6	18	MG dugout A.	E 22 b 2 2		16' cased passage 2 frames & lagging in dugout	4 frames out passage	
6	18	MG " B	E 22 bd 2		" "	" "	
6	18	MG " C	E 22 c 2 2		Passage & excavation 2 frames & lagging		

DATED p.m. 1916

Progress Report for 24 hours to pm. 1/8/16 1916

Reference to Map Sheet 57 D NE 1/10000

Number Employed		Nature of Work	At		Total Number of yards completed	Remaining to be done	Remarks
R.E.	Infantry		From	To.			
3	6	Baths Bienvillers	E 8 a 33				Completed.
1	-	Dug out HQ Northern Group	E 8 a 88.		12 passages 2 frames in.		
3	-	" . Bde HQ additions ~~addition~~ over + header	E 8 a 44		Framework erected & spiled & dogged		
1	-	" Backhow.			{1 gallery 15' {1 " 11'	20' to join	
4	8	Stokes gun dugout & emplacement	E 4 a 9.3		7 cases in		Material transported to site.
2	10	Wallis Huts well	D 22 c 26		120 cc taken out		
9	10	Huts	D 22 c	J. 3 a			4 huts taken down & transported
4	36	Specimen Firebays	Z 54 (Bde sector plan)				[illegible] excavated. Night shift occupied solely in clearing old work out of the way.

1/8/16

G. T. Rangsford
Maj. RE

Progress Report for 24 hours to 2 pm. 21.8.16. 1916.

Reference to Map Sheet 57 DNE. 1/10000

Number employed		Nature of Work	At		Total Number of yards completed.	Remaining to be done	Remarks.
RE.	Infantry.		From	To			
6	105	Regent St C.T. drainage	E21 b 15.15	E22 c 6.4 Brayelle Rd	900		3 shifts on all work round clock
-			E22 c 6.4	E22 d 05.15 Green street			All water out - trench cleared & dry for about 140 yds
		-	E22 d 05.15	E22 d 3 3 R. Dawson Lane			6" sludge in remainder
							Water being pumped & and cleared.
6	15	HQ dugout 'A'	E22 b 2 2		16' passage. ½ dugout roof frames & lagging	½ dugout track passage	
6	15	HQ " 'B'	E22 bd 2		" "	" "	
6	18	HQ " 'C'	E11 c 2 3		Passage & 3 frames & lagging		Clearing face in fault.
5	-	Dugout HQ Northern Group RFA					
		" Bde HQ	E11 44				Timbering & sheeting of new roof over all space completed

DATED . . . 1916 pm.

MAJOR R.E., T.,

O.C., 2nd/2nd LONDON FIELD CO.

Progress Report for 24 hours to 2 pm - - - - - 1916

Reference to Map - Sheet 1/10000

Number employed		Nature of Work.	At		Total Number of yards completed	Remaining to be done	Remarks
R.E.	Infantry		From	To			
1	RFA	Dugout BARKHOW					1 frame & 5 steps added.
1	RFA	Dugout HARGUN					3 frames & top lagging put in.
4	8	Stokes gun emplacement	E 11 a 9.3		11 cases in		
1	5	RFA 'OP'	E 16 a 9.3				Completed.
3	12	Coy H Q dugout	E 22 d 4.3 Rotten Lane		10' passage		Spoil has to be carried some distance to be got rid of.
3	12	Specimen firebays	E 22 d 4.1				1 Traverse cut & old trench blanked & revetted. Old partly cleaned.
4	10	H Q dugout			3' vertical shaft		Further 1'6" excavated at bottom
2	8	Valley Hut Wells	D 22 c 2.6				
9	10	Huts erection	J 3 a		Completed		

Dated. 2/8/ - - - 1916
9.45 p.m.

G. T. P. Hungerford
MAJOR R.E., T.,
O.C., 2nd/2nd LONDON FIELD CO.

Progress Report for 24 hours to . . pm . 31st Dec 1916

Reference to Map Sheet 57 D NE. 1/10000

Number Employed		Nature of Work	At		Total Number of yards completed	Remaining to be done	Remarks
R.E.	Infantry		From	To.			
7	120	Regent St C.T. drainage	E 21 b 15.15	E 22 d 05.15 Green Street	1300		Cleared of mud – No drainage arrangement yet begun
			E 22 d 05.10	E 22 d 33 Robinson Lane	100		Cleared.
6	15	HQ dugout A.	E 22 b 22		9'x9'6" excavation dugout – 3 frames lagged		
6	15	" " B	E 22 b d 2		9'x8'6 excavation dugout 2 frames & lagging		Fall of chalk has had to be cleared.
6	18	" " C	E 11 c 23		10'x9' excavation 4 frames & lagging		
2	.	Bde HQ dugout	E 8 a 44				Supervision of sandbagging & earth cover
1	RFA	Dugout BARISHOW	.				Assistance to RFA in fixing & repairing frames
1	"	Dugouts HARQUN	.		3 shafts 12' 6' horizontal gallery in each		

PROGRESS REPORT FOR 24 hours to ... p.m. .... 1916.

REFERENCE to MAP. SHEET. 1/10000.

Number employed: R.E.	Number employed: Infantry	Nature of Work	At: From	At: To	Total Number of yards completed	Remaining to be done.	Remarks.
4	8	Stokes gun dugout			15' down 14 cases in		Two shifts only. Transport of material takes considerable part of working time.
6	15	Coy HQ dugout	E 22 d 4.3		12' down 11 cases in.		
8	36	Specimen fire bays	E 22 d 4 1				One bay cleared out ready for firestep. One traverse cut out, 1 traverse ½ cut out. Special firestep to be fitted here
		MG dugout D	-		11 ft vertical shaft passed & lagged.		..
		OP Barkhow.	-				Completed.
2	8	Valley, Hut well.	D 22 c 2 6				Cleared & another frame down in.

Dated 3/8/1916

G. T. [illegible]
MAJOR R.E., T.,
O.C., 2nd/2nd LONDON FIELD CO.

Progress Report for 24 hours to 7pm 4/8/16 1916.

Reference to Map Sheet 1/10000

Number Employed		Nature of Work	At		Total Number of yards completed	Remaining to be done	Remarks
R.E.	Infantry		From	To			
3	50	Regent St C.T. clearing + drainage	E24 b 15.15	E22 d 05.15 Green St	1300		Party has been used entirely in salvaging R.E. material which [illegible] be got out ~~before~~ cleared out
			E22 d 05.15	E22 d 3.3 Robinson Lane			
4	12	HG dugout A	E22 b 22		Passage dugout	Cont 16'	2 shifts
4	12	" " B	E22 b d 2		"	Cont 16'	"
6	18	" " C	E4 c 23 E5 b				3 shifts
1	RFA	Dugouts HARGON	"				1 shift assistance [illegible] as labour available
2	"	" BARKHOS					
2	8	" Bde HQ	E[illegible]				
1	RAMC	" RAMC					
1	RFA	O.P. HARGON					Work [illegible] in [illegible].

Dated 4/8/ 1916
7.30 p.m.

MAJOR R.E., T.,
O.C., 2nd/2nd LONDON FIELD CO.

Progress Report for 24 hours to … 1916.

Number employed R.E.	Number employed Infantry	Nature of Work		Progress From	Progress To	Remarks
4	10	Stokes gun dugout & emplt.	E11a 9.3		Down shaft 15' 3' excavation dug.	2 shifts
4	10	Coy HQ dugout	E22d 4.3		15' passage cased	2 shifts.
5	24	Specimen fire bays	E22d 41			One traverse complete 5' high; " " " 3' 6' high; Night party clearing debris from parados.
4	10	HQ dugout .D.			15' put vertical shaft framed & lagged	2 shifts
4	8	III Army Intell. O.P.	"			Fitting & adapting instruments; 4 ft inclined shaft excavated & framed.
2	10	Valley Huts well	D22c 26		Completed	
4	5	Bastions lean to repair & window			"	
15	10	Dump & shops stores &c.				

Dated … 1916

G. T. Dempsey(?)
MAJOR R.E. T.,
O.C., 2nd/2nd LONDON FIELD CO.

PROGRESS REPORT FOR 24 HOURS [illegible] 9/10/16 .. 1916

Reference to Map - Sheet 57 D NE 1/10000.

Number employed		Nature of Work	From	To	Total Number of yards completed	[illegible] by hand	Remarks
R.E.	Infantry						
3	25	Regent St C.T. clearing, draining	E21b15.15	E22d05.15 Green St	1300		Cleared & dug - sumps not dug below Bengalla Rd
			E22cd1 Ribot Avenue	E22d32 R. Arundon	200		Cleared - no sumps dug.
6	18	MG dugout 'A'	E22b22	Entrance dugout 24ft cut	1st exit		
6	18	MG dugout 'B'	E22bd2	"	"		
6	18	MG dugout 'C'	E11c23	Entrance, dugout	exit passage		
1	RFA	Dugout MARGUN	E8 6		7' passage		Rain shift - assistance to labour available.
1	RFA	" BARBOON	E8 6				
3	-	" Bde HQ	E8a44				
4	8	Stokes gun dugout & emp.	E11a9.3	Entrance & 7' dugout excavated out. Temporary frames			
6	15	Coy HQ dugout	E22d4.3	Entrance passage 20'	dugout & exit.		

Dated

MAJOR R.E., T.,
O.C. 2nd/2nd LONDON FIELD CO.

Progress Report for 24 hours to pm – 1916.

Reference to Map Sheet 1/10000

Number Employed		Nature of Work	At		Total Number of yards completed	Remaining to be done	Remarks.
RE	Infantry		From	To.			
8	36	Spaceman fire bays	E22 d 4.1				Traverses complete 4' 6" high Bays cleaned. This work is being continued with special work.
6	18	MG dugout D.	E16 d 7 5		Entrance frames dugout sent to emplacement.		
3	12	III Army O.P.			8' entrance and framing.		
4	10	Hutting Gommecourt	D16 72		1 hut completed		1 hut taken down & transported to site
		Dump shops & sawmill					

5/81

G. T. Bungsford

MAJOR R.E., T.,
O.C., 2nd/2nd LONDON FIELD CO.

6th/2nd LONDON FIELD Co. R.E.

PROGRESS REPORT for 24 hours to 2 pm. . 6/5/. . 1916

Reference to Map Sheet 1/10000

Number Employed		Nature of Work.	At		Total Number of yards completed	Remaining to be done	Remarks.
R.E.	Infantry		From	To			

Date 1916

. . m.

Progress Report for 24 hours to 5pm 1916

Progress Report for 24 hours to 2pm 1916

Reference to Map Sheet [illegible] 1/10000

Number Employed		Nature of Work	At		Total Number of yards completed	Remaining to be done	Remarks
R.E.	Infantry		From	to			
3	12	[illegible] O.P.			[illegible]		[illegible]
4	[illegible]	[illegible]			[illegible]		

[illegible]

[illegible]

[illegible]

[illegible]

[illegible] Map Sheet [illegible]

Number Employed	Infantry	Nature of Work	From	To	Total number [illegible] completed	[illegible] done	Remarks
	–	Dugout [illegible]	E22 [illegible] E22 cd [illegible]	E22 d [illegible] E22 d 25	1200 200		Not work 2 shifts on account of [illegible] Parties [illegible]
4	12	M G dugout A			[illegible] dugout [illegible]	Emplacement	
4	12	" B			"	"	
4	12	" D	E22 d 75		Entrance & 3 frames of dugout	2 frames dugout & [illegible]	
1	RFA	Dugout [illegible]					Assistance as required to labour available
1	RFA	" RFA HQ					
2	–	" Bde HQ					
2	5	[illegible] dugout	E24 [illegible]		Entrance & 3 frames dugout	1 frame [illegible]	1 shift.
		[illegible] dugout	E22 d [illegible]				No report received.
4	12	MG dugout C	~~[illegible]~~ E22 d [illegible]		[illegible] dugout & 8' [illegible]	30 [illegible]	
2	5	[illegible] OP	"		1 [illegible] 18' [illegible]		
		[illegible]	D [illegible]		2 [illegible] complete		

[illegible] 7 8
9 30 p

G T [illegible]
Major [illegible]
OC 2/2 [illegible]

PROGRESS REPORT 7 a.m. to 2 p.m. 8/8/16 1916

Reference to Map Sheet 57 D

Number Employed R.E.	Number Employed Infantry	Nature of Work	At From	At To	Total Number of ... completed	Remaining to be done	Remarks
6	60	Roberts Avenue	E27a6.9	E22d9.5	–	–	From front line to Green St. trench boards taken up – trench cleaned out & deepened 1' – about 50 yds. Revetting with Trench elements & C.I. about 8 yds.
11	60	Green Street	E22c9.1 Roberts Av.	E22d3.3 Robinson Lane			50 yds cleared & 30 trench elements fixed
6	15	Stokes gun dugout emplacement	E11a9.3		Entrance & 11 frames	[illegible] frames	
6	15	M.G. dugout A	E22b2.2	–			1 Shaft down & complete
6	15	M.G. dugout B	E22b6.2	–			" " "
		M.G. dugout C	E11c2.3				
6	15	M.G. dugout D	E16d7.5		4 frames in & excavation for 4th.		Two heavy [illegible] encountered.
6	15	Coy H.Q. dugout Robinson Lane	E22d4.3		Entrance & two frames to dugout.		

Dated 1916

p.m.

4

2/1st LONDON FIELD CO. R.E.

Progress Report for 24 hours to 2pm ....1916.

Reference to Map Sheet 57 D. [illegible]

Number Employed		Nature of Work	[illegible]		Total Number of [illegible] completed	Remaining to be done	Remarks
	Infantry		[illegible]	[illegible]			
6	15	III Army OP	-		1st gallery 24		
4		OP HARGON			2nd " 6'		
		Doyle BARROW					24 concrete blocks cast & girders drilled.
		" Bde HQ					
2	-	Huts Gaudrempré					} as report [illegible]
4	-	Pump Souastre					To be completed tomorrow.
5	-	Latrines etc WARLINCOURT					Completed.
2		Church SOUASTRE					Indefinite amount of work
		Shops dump					Repairs to steel dowings

Progress Report … 24 hours to 2 pm. 9/8/ … 1916

Reference … Map Sheet … [illegible]

Number Employed		Nature of Work	A.		Total Number of … Completed	Remaining to be Done	Remarks
R. E.	Infantry		[illegible]	[illegible]			
	6	Robert Avenue [illegible]	E22a4 9	E22d 95	10		[illegible]
[illegible]	[illegible]	Cease St			36		[illegible]
6	15	[illegible]	E22a41	E22a 13			[illegible]
			E22 92		[illegible]		
[illegible]	[illegible]	[illegible] A					[illegible]
			E22 b22				Completed
6	[illegible]	[illegible]	E22b 82				
		[illegible]	E22c23		[illegible]		
6	[illegible]						
		[illegible]	E22d 70				
6	15						[illegible]
6	15	[illegible]			[illegible] 3		[illegible]
		[illegible]			[illegible]		[illegible]
					[illegible]		[illegible]
		[illegible]			[illegible]		

Passed … 1916

[illegible]

Reference to Map Sheet [illegible]

Number Employed		Nature of Work	At.		Total Number of yards completed	Remaining to be done	Remarks
R.E.	Infantry		From	To			
1	R.F.A.	Dugout Battery			[illegible]	[illegible]	1 [illegible]
2		[illegible] Gun [illegible]					Completed
		Latrines [illegible]					Completed
3		Trenching St. Amand			50 yds		
2	3	[illegible] [illegible] repair					[illegible]

Dated 1916

p.m.

Progress Report for 24 hours to 2 pm. 1916

Reference to Map Sheet [illegible]

Number Employed R.E.	Number Employed Infantry	Nature of Work	Co-ordinates From	Co-ordinates To	Total Number of yards completed	Remaining to be done	Remarks
6	60	Reb[illegible] Avenue – reclamation [illegible]	[illegible]	[illegible]	30 yds		Duckwalks lifted [illegible] drains [illegible] [illegible]
6	60	Green Street	E22 c 9.1	E22 a 2.3	30 yds		" "
6	15	Strong point dugout emplacement	F11 a 9.3				No report
6	15	M.G. dugout C	F11 c 2.3		Entrance dugout 10' exit	6' exit completed	
6	15	" " D	E11 a 7.5		Entrance & 4 frames & dugout excavated & 4 frames	exit & [illegible] completed	
6	15	Coy H.Q.	E22 a 4.3		1 entrance & 3 frames. Exit excavated 20 ft. Entrance 19'. Entrance & exit		
3	R.E.	O.P. dugout [illegible]					Excavation of dugout begun
		" " [illegible]					
		III Army O.P. 1.			Entrance [illegible]		Exit falling 7' [illegible] no working party [illegible]
		" " " 2.					Brown plaster lined [illegible]; floor cleared
		[illegible] St. [illegible]					[illegible] post [illegible] stopped [illegible]
		Chalk [illegible]					Completed
		Pump					[illegible]
		Stopping post					

Dated 11/8/1916
10 a.m.

G T [illegible]
[illegible]

Progress Report ... 2 ... 12/8 – 1916

Reference to Map Sheet 57 D NE.

Number Employed		Nature of Work	Map Ref.		Total ... yards	Remaining			Remarks
R 6	COWRIKY	Robert Avenue – reclamation & repair	E28 ab 9.1	E28 d 9.5 15	50				24x duckboards laid · with revetting
6	60	Green street	E22 e 9.1	E22 d 2.3	58				10 yds trench cleared 28x duckwalks laid 7 yds trench cleared
6	15	S15th Gun emplacement	E11 a 9.3				Entrance to dugout	Exit to emplacement	
3	15	MG dugout C	E11 c 2.3				Entrance & dugout 16' exit	Emplacement	
6	15	" " D	E16 d 7.5				Entrance & 5 frames to dugout		Excavated for 6' frame
		Coy HQ dugout	E22 d 4.3				Entrance & 3 frames 2' exit from top	3 frames to dugout & exit	
6	15	Infantry dugout							Delayed owing to men being taken for props.
6	RFA	OP & dugout HARGUN	E11a 8.5 3.0						Work set out & 3 frames to entrance.
			–				Entrance 11 frames exit 2 frames Entrance exit		
1	RFA	dugout BARROW							1 frame to dugout.
2	–	III Army OP 1							Side bracing stepping entrance
2		" " 2					Completed		
2		" " 3							
3	.	Horse troughs St AMAND Shops & dump					22.		Entrance trench cut & 1 frame in.

ed 12/8/16 ... 1916

G.T. Plungsford Lt

Progress Report for 24 hours to 2 pm 1916

2 13 8 16

Reference to Map Sheet 1/20000 57 D NE

Number Employed: R.E.	Infantry &c	Nature of Work	At: From	to	Total number of yards completed	Remaining to be done		Remarks
		Green Street	E22c9.1	E22d.2.3		60		18 yds sandbagging above revetment
6	60	Roberts Avenue	E28a6.9	E21d 9.5.15		55.		20 yds sandbagging.
6	15	Stokes Gun emplacement	E11a9.3		Entrance & dugout			Dugout lagged two cases & 2 cases in L. exit
3	15	MG dugout 'C'	E11c2.3		Entrance dugout & 13 frames exit		2 frames emplacement.	
6	15	" " 'D'	E16d7.5		Entrance & dugout			Exit begun.
6	15	Coy HQ dugout	E22d4.3		Entrance & 4 frames to dugout.			
6	15	Infantry dugout	E11a8.3		9 cases to Entrance			2nd entrance 8 cyds excavated
3	RFO	Dugout OP HARROW			1 gallery.		dugout & ½ exit	2nd gallery four frames
2	"	Dugout Barrow			entrance & exit			1 special 9' frame to dugout; 1 shift
		III Army OP's						Working parties report [illegible]
1	6	Sluggers Post	E22d5.4					23 c yds excavated
3	-	[illegible] St ROLAND				30.		1 baby elephant [illegible] } 1 shift
		Slopes dump.						About 30 yds trenching [illegible]

[illegible]

[illegible] REPORT [illegible] 1916

Reference to Map Sheet 44 / 8 / 1/10000 16

57 d NE

Number Employed		Nature of Work.	From		Total Number of yards completed	Remaining to be done		Remarks
R	INFANTRY		from	to				
4	60	Roberts Avenue – drainage & repairs	E28 a 6.9	E29 a 45.15		70		240 yds trench cleared and 80 elements in position
4	60	Green Street " "	E22 c 8.1	E22 d 2.3		70		28 yds cleared & 3 elements placed
6	15	Stokes gun emplacement	E4 c 9.3		Entrance to dugout		exit	3 [illegible] & exit
3	15	MG dugout 'C'	E4 c 2.3		Entrance dugout		exit & emplacement	2' of exit only to reach emplacement
6	15	" " 'D'	E16 d 7.5		"		"	6' exit gallery
6	15	Coy HQ dugout	E22 d 4.3		Entrance & 5 frames to dugout			2nd entrance 10' down
9	15	Infantry dugout	E11 a 8.3		15' cases to entrance			position cleared for 2nd entrance
6	RFA	Dugout for OP HARGON	–		1 entrance			9' horizontal heading for dugout 12' 2nd entrance
1	RFA	" [illegible]			Entrance reset framed			1 frame to dugout 90 c ft excavated for 2nd frame
		III Army OPs						No report in.
5	18	Regent Street – sumps			10 sumps were revetted			
1	12	Stragglers post	E22 d 8.4		100 yds excavated.			
3	–	Horse troughs St AMAND			2 troughs			About 14 yds troughing to be done
		Stopes & dump						

Dated 1916
14/8/16

G T [illegible]

Progress Report from ... to 2 pm ... 1916

Reference Map Sheet 57 D N.E. 2 15 / 18 / 6

Number Employed: R.E.	Infantry	Nature of Work	From	To	Total Number of yards completed	Remaining to be done		Remarks
		Roberts Avenue - repairs & drainage	E 22 a 4 9	to E 22 a ...	86			No more trench cleared
4	64	Green Street	E 22 c 9.1	E 22 a 2.3	90			All men on completing what is begun.
6	15	Stokes gun emplacement & dugout	E 11 c 9.3					12 [illegible] carried in by miners
3	15	M.G. dugout 'C'	E 11 c 2.3		Entrance & dugout, entrance dugout [illegible]		Emplacement framing	7 cases to exit
6	15	" " 'D'	E 16 d 7.5					3 frames in to exit.
6	15	Coy HQ dugout	E 22 d 4.3		Entrance & dugout			Exit 10' down
10	15	Infantry dugout	E 11 a 8.3		Entrance & 3 frames shelter to dugout			
6	RFA	Dugout for HARROW	—		13 cases 1st gallery, 3 cases 2nd gallery, 2 galleries. 11' horizontal heading to dugout			
1	–	" ARROW			Entrance & exit frames			
3	18	III by O.P. (b)	VIENNA TRENCH		1st gallery complete			120 ft chalk excavated to dugout
		" " 10	E 25 c 3.5		10' entrance trench			2nd gallery 10' down & trench to O.P. 3' in.
		III Army O.P. (A)	Château de la Haie		6' incline gallery Completed			Camouflage, shelter & false floor for instrument & operation.
3	4	Regent Street Sumps			Completed			

Dated 1916

G. T. Pringsford

Progress Report for 24 hours to 2 pm 1916

Reference to Map Sheet 1/10000

Number Employed		Nature of Work.	From	To	Total Number of yards completed	Remaining to be done		Remarks
R.E.	Infantry							
4	2	[illegible] Avenue – repairs + drainage	E28 c 6.9	E24 d 5.5	79	done		1 shift only reported on account of Bde relief
2	2	Gun Street	E22 c 4.1	E22 d 2.3	77			~~[illegible]~~
2	5	Slopes from emplacement	E4 a 4.3		Entrance dugout Exit		Emplacement	1½ working parties on [illegible] shaft Exit 10 ft
		HQ dugout C	E4 c 2.3					
2	5	HQ dugout D	E10 d 7.5		Entrance + dugout ~~[illegible]~~			
2	5	Coy HQ dugout	E22 d 4.3		Entrance + 5 frames dugout			4 frames to exit + tunnelling through for air passage
3	10	Infantry dugout	E4 a 8.3		20 frames 1st gall 3 " 2nd "			4' excavation for landing.
2	RFA	Dugout + OP [illegible]	.		2 galleries		10' [illegible] landing	13' temporary gallery through
1	"	" [illegible]	.		Entrance rock [illegible] 1 gallery complete			2 frames to dugout 2nd gallery 12' connecting gallery 5'
3	2	III Army OP (b)	Vienna Trench					
3	8	" (c)	E25 c 3.5		Entrance trench 10' inclined gallery			

G. T. [illegible]

Dated 1916

[illegible]

PROGRESS REPORT ... 2 ... 17/8/1916

57 D NE.

Number Employed		Nature of Work	Map reference		Work done		Remarks
RE	Infantry						
4	60	Roberts Avenue repair & drainage	E28 a b g	E21 d 95.15	95		
4	60	Green Street	E22 c 9 1	E22 d 2.3	DO		Post cramped excavation for about 12 yds
6	15	Stokes Gun emplacement	E11 a 9.3		Entrance dugout Exit "	" emplacement	20 c ft excavation ...
3	10	MG dugout C	E11 c 2.3				
6	15	" " D	E16 d 7.5		Entrance dugout	Exit emplacement	16' exit gallery through
6	15	Coy HQ dugout	E22 d 4.3		Entrance & 6 frames to dugout		air passage through
10	15	Infantry dugout	E11 a 8.3.		24 [illegible] 1st gall. " 2nd gall.		
6	RFA	Dugout & OP HARGUN	-		2 shafts & joining gallery	dugout	
		" BARKHOW.	-		Entrance exit 2 frames dugout	4 frames dugout	
		III Army OP (b)					} no report
		" " " (c)					
2	12	Stragglers post Horse trough St Amand	E22 d 8 4		practically complete Completed		

G T Pringle[?]

Dated 1916

b.m.

56th Divisional Engineers

2/2nd LONDON FIELD COMPANY R. E.

SEPTEMBER 1916.

56 Div

Instructions regarding War Diaries and Intelligence Summaries are contained in F. S. Regs., Part II. and the Staff Manual respectively. Title Pages will be prepared in manuscript.

WAR DIARY
or
INTELLIGENCE SUMMARY
(Erase heading not required.)

2/2nd London F^d Co RE

Vol 7

Army Form C. 2118

Place	Date	Hour	Summary of Events and Information	Remarks and references to Appendices
NEUF MOULIN	1/9/16		NIL	G.T.K
"	2/9/16		4 O.R. Evacuated. The Company Transport left NEUF MOULIN for CORBIE under command of CAPT. F.R. UNWIN	G.T.K
"	3/9/16		The dismounted portion of Company entrained at St RIQUIER for CORBIE under command of MAJOR G.T. KINGSTORD, with the 169th BRIGADE	G.T.K
CORBIE	4/9/16		Company moved with 169 BRIGADE into bivouacs behind XIV CORPS front	G.T.K
HAPPY VALLEY CAMP	5/9/16		NIL	G.T.K
			Moved to BRONFOY FARM CAMP TRANSPORT at CITADEL	G.T.K
BRONFOY FARM	6/9/16		Company started work on MINE DUGOUTS for battle Headquarters north of ANGLE WOOD	G.T.K
"	7/9/16		NIL	G.T.K
"	8/9/16			
"	9/9/16		No 3 Section Lt Beit & 2/Lt Small attached 169th INFANTRY BRIGADE for consolidation in connection with attack to NORTH & EAST of LEUZE WOOD. Half the section LT BEIT carried out this work on the NORTH. R.E. assistance for consolidation on EAST for which 2/Lt SMALL detailed not called for. 2 O.R Wounded. 1 O.R. slightly wounded "at duty" 1 O.R Wounded & missing	G.T.K
"	10/9/16		NIL	G.T.K
"	11/9/16		NIL. 1. O.R. Evacuated	G.T.K
"	12/9/16		10. O.Rs joined Unit from BASE	G.T.K

W. W. . . ./826 1,000,000 . . . I.B.C. & A. A.D.S.S./Forms/C. 2118.

Instructions regarding War Diaries and Intelligence Summaries are contained in F. S. Regs., Part II. and the Staff Manual respectively. Title Pages will be prepared in manuscript.

WAR DIARY
or
INTELLIGENCE SUMMARY
(Erase heading not required.)

Army Form C. 2118

Place	Date	Hour	Summary of Events and Information	Remarks and references to Appendices
BRONFOY FARM CAMP	13-9-16		NIL	GTK
"	14-9-16		Company moved to BATTLE HEADQUARTERS N.E. of FAVIÉRE WOOD	GTK
	"		+ transport moved from CITADEL to BRONFOY FARM CAMP	
BATTLE H.Qs	15-9-16		4 Sections of Sappers proceeded with 2 Companies of the 1/5th Cheshire Regiment at a.m. to continue track from Angle Wood, by FALFEMONT FARM to S.W. corner of LEUZE WOOD, but were not able to work at track owing to heavy enemy fire, and returned to BATTLE HEADQUARTERS at 7.0 PM	GTK
"	16-9-16		Bivouaced at BATTLE HEADQUARTERS awaiting orders	GTK
	17-9-16		No 2 Section 2/Lt BOURNE employed night work improving loop trench and wiring in front of it. No 4 Section employed constructing STRONG POINT at T.27 c 4.8.	GTK
	18-9-16		No 1 Section reported at BRIGADE H.Q. for duty in consolidating new trenches to be attacked by 169th BRIGADE but they were not called upon for work. No. 3. Section employed night work continuing STRONG POINT at T 27. c 4.8 begun by No 2 Section on the 17th inst.	GTK
	19-9-16		No. 2 Section employed night work in completing STRONG POINT at T.27 c 4.8. No 4 Section employed night work in constructing STRONG POINT at T 27. a 0.8. & Nos 1 & 3 Sections employed in digging new FIRE TRENCH from T27. a 0.8 to T27. b. 1.6. 3 ORs Wounded. 5 ORs joined from BASE	GTK

1875 Wt. W593/826 1,000,000 4/15 J.B.C. & A. A.D.S.S./Forms/C. 2118.

Instructions regarding War Diaries and Intelligence Summaries are contained in F. S. Regs., Part II. and the Staff Manual respectively. Title Pages will be prepared in manuscript.

WAR DIARY
or
INTELLIGENCE SUMMARY
(Erase heading not required.)

Army Form C. 2118

Place	Date	Hour	Summary of Events and Information	Remarks and references to Appendices
BATTLE HEADQUARTERS	20/9/16		No 2 Section employed night work in improving STRONG POINT at T27 b 1.4 and in constructing Company Headquarters at about B 2 c 2.3	GJK
	21/9/16		1 O.R. KILLED 2 O.Rs WOUNDED No 1 & 4 Section employed in wiring new trench from LEUZE WOOD to Loop trench ~~[illegible]~~	GJK
	22/9/16		No 2 Section completed wiring commenced on 21st. No 3 Section on digging T head in advance of LEUZE WOOD to LOOP TRENCH	GJK
	23/9/16		~~No 2 Section employed deepening & completing STRONG POINT at T27 b 1.5. and~~ NIL.	GJK
	24/9/16		No 1 & 3 Section employed in constructing Battn H.Q. Dugouts at FALFEMONT FARM	GJK
	25/9/16		1 O.R. Wounded. Nos 2 & 4 Section sent forward to ANGLE WOOD to await orders from BRIGADE. No 3 Section employed in completing Battn Dugouts near FALFEMONT FARM	GJK
	26/9/16		5 O.R. Joined from BASE. Nos 2 & 4 Section employed constructing trench from Angle WOOD to FALFEMONT FARM. No 1 SECTION completed the work at night	GJK
	27/9/16		Dismounted portion of Company moved from Battle H.Q to MEAULTE under command of Major G.T Kingsford	GJK
MEAULTE	28/9/16		Remainder of Company moved from BRONFAY FARM CAMP to MEAULTE under Command of Capt F.R. UNWIN	GJK
MEAULTE	29/9/16		Company less transport moved from MEAULTE ~~[illegible]~~ & bivouaced N.E of CARNOY under command of Major G.T KINGSFORD Transport moved from MEAULTE to Lines W. of BRICQUETERIE A.4.a	GJK
	30/9/16		Dismounted portion of Company under command of OC moved to Battle H.Q. W of TRONES WOOD S.24 d.11.	GJK

G.T Kingsford Major RE

1875 Wt. W593/826 1,000,000 4/15 J.B.C. & A. A.D.S.S./Forms/C. 2118.

Instructions regarding War Diaries and Intelligence Summaries are contained in F. S. Regs., Part II. and the Staff Manual respectively. Title Pages will be prepared in manuscript.

WAR DIARY
or
INTELLIGENCE SUMMARY
(Erase heading not required.)

Army Form C. 2118

2nd/2nd LONDON FIELD CO. R.E.

Place	Date	Hour	Summary of Events and Information	Remarks and references to Appendices
BERNAFAY WOOD	9/10/16		Dismounted portion of Company moved from BERNAFAY WOOD to CITADEL Transport moved from BRIQUETERIE to MANSEL CAMP	GIK
CITADEL	10/10/16		Dismounted personnel under Capt UNWIN moved by Motor Bus to YSEAUX. Transport moved from MANSEL CAMP to BUSSY-LES-DOUARS, under O.C	[illegible]
YSEAUX	11/10/16		Transport by road under O.C to YSEAUX. 6 O.R. joined from BASE.	GIK
"	12/10/16		Company in Rest Billets.	[illegible]
"	13/10/16		Do	[illegible]
"	14/10/16		Do.	[illegible] GIK
"	15/10/16		Do	[illegible]
"	16/10/16		Do 6 ORs joined from BASE	[illegible]
"	17/10/16		Do	[illegible]
"	18/10/16		Do	GIK
"	19/10/16		Do	
"	20/10/16		Do.	GIK

1875 Wt. W593/826 1,000,000 4/15 J.B.C. & A. A.D.S.S./Forms/C. 2118.

Instructions regarding War Diaries and Intelligence Summaries are contained in F. S. Regs., Part II. and the Staff Manual respectively. Title Pages will be prepared in manuscript.

WAR DIARY
or
INTELLIGENCE SUMMARY
(Erase heading not required.)

Army Form C. 2118

2nd/2nd LONDON FIELD CO. R.E.

Place	Date	Hour	Summary of Events and Information	Remarks and references to Appendices
ERONDELLE.	21/10/16		Company moved under Command of O.C. from YSEUX to ERONDELLE.	GJK.
	22/10/16		NIL	GJK
	23/10/16		NIL	T.P.C
CALONNE.	24/10/16		Entrained at PONT REMY and detrained at BERGETTE. marched to CALONNE-SUR-LY-LYS	T.P.C
	25/10/16		NIL	GJK
	26/10/16		NIL	T.P.C
	27/10/16		NIL	T.P.C
8 MAISONS.	28/10/16		Company moved from CALONNE to HUIT MAISONS under O.C.	GJK
"	29/10/16		Reconnaissance by Officers & NCOs on work to be undertaken & improvement of billets.	GJK
	30/10/16		No2 Section begun work on parapet of front line left sector & No4 Section on work on parapet of front line right sector. No 1 section on work on B. line switch. No.3 section on Artillery O.Ps. & construction of Brigade drying room	T.P.C
	31/10/16		Do Do Do Do Do.	T.P.C

C. I. Dingsford[?] Maj. RE.

2nd/2nd LONDON FIELD CO. R.E.

Instructions regarding War Diaries and Intelligence Summaries are contained in F. S. Regs., Part II. and the Staff Manual respectively. Title Pages will be prepared in manuscript.

WAR DIARY
or
INTELLIGENCE SUMMARY
(Erase heading not required.)

Army Form C. 2118

2/2 London Fd Coy
Vol 9

Place	Date	Hour	Summary of Events and Information	Remarks and references to Appendices
HUIT MAISONS	1/11/16		Work continued in Left Right Sector of BRIGADE FRONT, also on B LINE + O.Ps	GJK
	2/11/16		Do Do Do Do	GJK
	3/11/16		Do Do Do Do 1 O.R. Evacuated to C.C.S.	GJK
	4/11/16		Work continued in Left Right Sector of BRIGADE FRONT, B.LINE + O.Ps. 1 O.R. Evac to C.C.S.	GJK
	5/11/16		Do Do Do Do 3 O.Rs to Hospital	GJK
	6/11/16		Do Do Do Do. LIEUT R.O. BEIT rejoined from LEAVE	[illegible]
	7/11/16		1 O.R. to Hospital Work continued in Left Right Sector of BRIGADE FRONT, B LINE + O.Ps etc	GJK
	8/11/16		Do Do Do Do	[illegible]
	9/11/16		Do Do Do Do 2 O.Rs to Hospital 1 O.R. left on Leave	[illegible]
	10/11/16		1 O.R. rejoined UNIT from attachment to Divisional RE. Work continued as usual.	GJK
	11/11/16		No 4 Section under command of 2/LIEUT DAIN moved to MERVILLE for work in Divisional Schools No 2 Section work on SCREENS 2 O.R. evacuated	GJK
	12/11/16		Ordinary Routine of Work in Front Line, Back Areas, Screens etc	GJK

1875 Wt. W593/826 1,000,000 4/15 J.B.C. & A. A.D.S.S./Forms/C. 2118.

Instructions regarding War Diaries and Intelligence Summaries are contained in F. S. Regs., Part II. and the Staff Manual respectively. Title Pages will be prepared in manuscript.

WAR DIARY
or
INTELLIGENCE SUMMARY
(Erase heading not required.)

Army Form C. 2118

Place	Date	Hour	Summary of Events and Information	Remarks and references to Appendices
HUIT MAISONS	13/11/16		Ordinary Routine of Work in Front Line. Back Areas etc. 1 O.R to Hospital.	GTK
	14/11/16		Do Do Do 1. O.R to " 1 O.R. Evacuated	GTK
	15/11/16		Do Do Do 1. O.R. proceeded on Leave.	GTK
	16/11/16		Do Do Do 2 O.Rs to Hospital 1 O.R joined from BASE.	GTK
	17/11/16		No 1 Section resting. No 4 Section moved from MERVILLE to HUIT MAISON. Lt R.O BEIT left for 1st ARMY SCHOOL as Instructor. 2 O.Rs joined from Hospital 1. O.R joined from BASE.	GTK
	18/11/16		No 1 Section took over work on Tramways under the Divisional Tramway Officer. Nos 2 & 3 Sections resting 1. O.R to Hospital 1. O.R. Evacuated.	[illegible]
	19/11/16		No 2 Section took over work in Front Line & No 3 took over work in Back Area	[illegible]
	20/11/16		Ordinary Routine of Work in Front Line, Back Areas etc. 1 O.R rejoined from C.R.S. 1 O.R. evacuated	GTK
	21/11/16		Do Do Do Do	[illegible]
	22/11/16		Do Do Do Do	[illegible]
	23/11/16		Do Do Do Do 9 O.Rs joined from BASE	GTK
	"		Capt UNWIN rejoined from appointment of Adjutant Divl. R.E. 1. O.R rejoined from LEAVE.	
	24/11/16		Ordinary Routine of Work in Front Line Back Areas etc. 3 O.Rs left for Leave	GTK
	25/11/16		Do Do Do Do	GTK
	26/11/16		Nos 2 & 3 Sections resting.	GTK
	27/11/16		No 2 Section moved to NOUVEAU MONDE for work in C.R.E. YARDS & various jobs	[illegible]

Army Form C. 2118

Instructions regarding War Diaries and Intelligence Summaries are contained in F. S. Regs., Part II. and the Staff Manual respectively. Title Pages will be prepared in manuscript.

WAR DIARY
or
INTELLIGENCE SUMMARY
(Erase heading not required.)

Place	Date	Hour	Summary of Events and Information	Remarks and references to Appendices
HUIT MAISON	28/11/16		Change of Sector. New Sector extending from CHURCH ROAD to TILLELOY SOUTH taken over from 1/1st EDINBURGH FIELD Coy, and old Sector, extending from Bond Street to Church Road handed over to 1/2nd LOWLAND FIELD Coy. No 1 & 3 Sections commenced work in new Sector on front line & CTs. No 4 Section commenced work in back areas.	GJK.
	29/11/16		Ordinary Routine	GJK
	30/11/16		Ordinary Routine. 3 ORs joined from BASE. 1 OFFICER & 2 ORs left for leave.	

G. T. [illegible] Maj-RE
OC 2/2nd Lowland Fd Co RE

1875 Wt. W593/826 1,000,000 4/15 J.B.C. & A. A.D.S.S./Forms/C. 2118.

Secret

Vol 10

Army Form C. 2118

WAR DIARY
or
INTELLIGENCE SUMMARY
(Erase heading not required.)

Instructions regarding War Diaries and Intelligence Summaries are contained in F. S. Regs., Part II. and the Staff Manual respectively. Title Pages will be prepared in manuscript.

2/2nd London Field Co RE

Place	Date	Hour	Summary of Events and Information	Remarks and references to Appendices
HUIT MAISON	1/12/16		Work continued in New Sector – CHURCH ROAD to TILLELOY SOUTH.	T.D.C.
	2/12/16		Work continued in Do. No 4 Section working in BACK AREA.	T.D.C.
	3/12/16		Do Do. Do	T.D.C.
	4/12/16		Do Do Do	T.D.C.
	5/12/16		Do Do Do 3 O.Rs rejoined from Leave. 3 O.Rs left Company on Leave 1 O.R. admitted to Hospital	T.D.C.
	6/12/16		Work continued in CHURCH Road to TILLELOY SOUTH. 1 O.R. Rejoined from Hospital	G.T.K.
	7/12/16		Do Do. Do	G.T.K.
	8/12/16		No 2 Section returned from NOUVEAU MONDE Nos 1 & 3 Sections in FRONT LINE & No 4 Section in BACK AREAS 1 O.R. admitted to Hospital	G.T.K.
	9/12/16		Rest day for Company.	G.T.K.
	10/12/16		No 1 Section took over work from No 4 Section in Support. Nos 2 & 4 Sections took over work in Front Line. No 3 Section under command of Lt SMAIL moved to MERVILLE.	T.D.C.
	11/12/16		Work continued ~~in~~ FRONT LINE. BACK AREAS etc. 1 OFFICER 2/Lt BOURNE & 2 O.Rs left Company for 10 days leave	T.D.C.

1875 Wt. W593/826 1,000,000 4/15 J.B.C. & A. A.D.S.S./Forms/C. 2118.

Instructions regarding War Diaries and Intelligence Summaries are contained in F. S. Regs., Part II. and the Staff Manual respectively. Title Pages will be prepared in manuscript.

WAR DIARY
or
INTELLIGENCE SUMMARY
(Erase heading not required.)

Army Form C. 2118

Place	Date	Hour	Summary of Events and Information	Remarks and references to Appendices
HUIT MAISON	12/2/16		Work continued in FRONT LINE in SUPPORT & at MERVILLE. 2 ORs to Hospital.	GJK
	13/2/16		Do Do Do Do 1 OFFICER 2/Lt DAIN & 2 O.Rs rejoined from LEAVE.	GJK
	14/2/16		Work continued in FRONT LINE by Nos 2 & 4 Sections No 1 Section in Support & No 3 Section at MERVILLE	GJK
	15/2/16		Do Do Do Do	GJK
	16/2/16		Do Do Do Do 3 ORs proceeded on leave. O.C. left Company to act for CRE 58 Divn	CHRD
	17/2/16		Do Do Do 1 ORs to hospital	CHRD
	18/2/16		Do Do Do	CHRD
	19/2/16		Do Do Do	CHRD
	20/2/16		Do Do Do Orders received for Company to move to new Billets at LAVENTIE. No 1 Section moved to LAVENTIE to prepare billets	CHRD
LAVENTIE	21/2/16		Company less No 1 & No 3 Section moved to LAVENTIE under command of CAPT UNWIN. No 3 Section under command of Lt Snail moved from MERVILLE to LAVENTIE. 1 OFFICER Lt VILLA & 2 ORs left for leave	CHRD

1875 Wt. W593/826 1,000,000 4/15 J.B.C. & A. A.D.S.S./Forms/C. 2118.

Instructions regarding War Diaries and Intelligence Summaries are contained in F. S. Regs., Part II. and the Staff Manual respectively. Title Pages will be prepared in manuscript.

WAR DIARY
or
INTELLIGENCE SUMMARY
(Erase heading not required.)

Army Form C. 2118

Place	Date	Hour	Summary of Events and Information	Remarks and references to Appendices
LAVENTIE	22/12/16		Work begun in New Sector from Sign Post Lane to Winchester St. No 3 section on right subsection & No 2 on 'R' line. No 4 on tramways & No 1 working on billets. O.C returned from duty at D.H.Q	G.T.K
"	23/12/16		Work as on 22/12/16 1 OR evacuated to hospital self inflicted wound.	G.T.K.
"	24/12/16		No 1 section started work on left subsector – Lt Bourne returned from leave 2Lt [illegible]	G.T.K
"	25/12/16		Work continued – half day granted by G.O.C. 1 OR returned from hospital	G.T.K
"	26/12/16		Work continued. 1 OR returned from hospital	G.T.K
"	27/12/16		" " 2 OR returned from leave 1 OR returned from Hospital – Capt F.R. Unwin to Hospital Lt Pennock & 4 OR proceeded on leave	G.T.K
"	28/12/16		Work continued – 1 OR returned from leave 2 OR to Hospital	G.T.K
"	29/12/16		Work continued – 3 OR to Hospital 1 OR rejoined from Hospital	G.T.K
"	30/12/16		" " 1 OR to Hospital	G.T.K
"	31/12/16		" " 1 OR killed 1 OR wounded	G.T.K

C.T. Kingsford
Maj – R.E.

1875 Wt. W593/826 1,000,000 4/15 J.B.C. & A. A.D.S.S./Forms/C. 2118.

Instructions regarding War Diaries and Intelligence Summaries are contained in F. S. Regs., Part II. and the Staff Manual respectively. Title Pages will be prepared in manuscript.

WAR DIARY
or
INTELLIGENCE SUMMARY
(Erase heading not required.)

Army Form C. 2118

51 3/2 Fd Coy RE

Vol 12

Place	Date	Hour	Summary of Events and Information	Remarks and references to Appendices
LAVENTIE	1/1/17		Work continued in Sign Post Lane to Winchester St 1 O.R. rejoined from Hospital.	GJK
"	2/1/17		Rest day for Company. Inspection of Kit, Rifles etc carried out also Respirator Drill 3 O.R. proceeded on Leave. 1 OFFICER + 2 O.R. rejoined from leave 2 O.R. rejoined from Hospital	GJK
"	3/1/17		Nos 2 + 4 Section took over work in Front Line from Nos 1 + 3 Sections. No 3 Section took over work in R. Line from No 3 Section No 1 Section moved to NOUVEAU MONDE 1 O.R. evacuated 1 O.R. to Hospital	GJK
"	4/1/17		Work continued by Sections as on 3rd inst 1 O.R. wounded	GJK
"	5/1/17		" " " " " " " " 1 O.R. to Hospital	GJK
"	6/1/17		" " " " " " " " 1 O.R. to Hospital	GJK
"	7/1/17		" " " " 1 OFFICER + 2 O.R. proceeded on Leave 1 O.R. rejoined from Hospital	GJK
"	8/1/17		" " " " 1 OFFICER + 3 O.R. rejoined from Leave	GJK
"	9/1/17		" " " " 2 O.R. to Hospital.	GJK
"	10/1/17		" " " "	GJK
"	11/1/17		" " 1 O.R. Joined from BASE 1 O.R. rejoined from Hospital	GJK

1375 Wt. W593/826 1,000,000 4/15 J.B.C. & A. A.D.S.S./Forms/C. 2118.

Instructions regarding War Diaries and Intelligence Summaries are contained in F. S. Regs., Part II. and the Staff Manual respectively. Title Pages will be prepared in manuscript.

WAR DIARY
or
INTELLIGENCE SUMMARY
(Erase heading not required.)

Army Form C. 2118

Place	Date	Hour	Summary of Events and Information	Remarks and references to Appendices
LAVENTIE	12/1/17		Work continued in FRONT LINE. SUPPORT LINE + at NOUVEAU MONDE. 4 ORs proceeded on Leave. 1 OR rejoined from Hospital	GIK
	13/1/17		Work continued No 1 Section moved from NOUVEAU MONDE to LAVENTIE.	GIK
	14/1/17		Company Rest day. Inspection of Rifles, Equipment Clothing etc. and Gas Respirator drill carried out 1 OR to Hospital	GIK
	15/1/17		Nos 1 + 3 Sections took over work from Nos 2 & 4 Section in FRONT LINE No 4 Section took over work in SUPPORT LINE from No 3 Section No 2 Section moved to MERVILLE under command of 2/Lt BOURNE. 1 OR to Hospital	GIK
	16/1/17		Work continued in Front Line Support Line & at Merville Lt BEIT + 1 O.R. rejoined from 1st ARMY SCHOOL 2/Lt PINNOCK H.G + 2/Lt MACFARLANE M. left the Company on being transferred to Heavy Machine Gun Branch	
	17/1/17		Work continued 1 Officer + 2 O.Rs proceeded on Leave	
	18/1/17		" " 1 " + 2 ORs rejoined from Leave	
	19/1/17		" " 1 NCO + 2 ORs operated with Infantry in Raid on enemy trenches and attempted to damage the enemy wire with Bangalore Torpedoes. The attempt was not successful owing to heavy enemy fire 1 OR joined from Base 1 OR rejoined from Hospital	

1375 Wt. W593/826 1,000,000 4/15 J.B.C. & A. A.D.S.S./Forms/C. 2118.

Instructions regarding War Diaries and Intelligence Summaries are contained in F. S. Regs., Part II. and the Staff Manual respectively. Title Pages will be prepared in manuscript.

WAR DIARY
or
INTELLIGENCE SUMMARY
(Erase heading not required.)

Army Form C. 2118

Place	Date	Hour	Summary of Events and Information	Remarks and references to Appendices
LAVENTIE	19/1/17		MAJOR KINGSFORD G.T. & 1 O.R. proceeded to RE School of Instruction 1 O.R. Wounded.	G.G.J.
	20/1/17		Work continued 1 O.R. to Hospital	G.G.J.
	21/1/17		" "	G.G.J.
	22/1/17		" " 3 O.Rs proceeded on leave 3 O.Rs rejoined from leave.	G.G.J.
	23/1/17		" " 1 O.R. Killed 2 O.Rs Wounded.	G.G.J.
	24/1/17		" "	G.G.J.
	25/1/17		No 2 Section moved from ~~[illegible]~~ MERVILLE to LAVENTIE under command of Lt BOURNE. Company Rest day. Rifle Kit & Respirators inspected & drill carried out.	G.G.J.
	26/1/17		Nos 2 & 4 Sections relieved Nos 1 & 3 in FRONT LINE. No 1 relieved No 4 in R Line. No 3 Section took over work on Tramways ~~[illegible]~~ 2 O.Rs to Hospital	G.G.J.
	27/1/17		Work continued as above	G.G.J.
	28/1/17		" " " " Lt PINNOCK & Lt MACFARLANE rejoined from Heavy M.G. Branch	G.G.J.
	29/1/17		" " " " No 4 Section moved to NOUVEAU MONDE to relieve 416 Fd Co owing to redistribution of RE work in Line. Work in Line handed over to 416 Field Co RE.	G.G.J.
	30/1/17		Sections employed on Divisional Screens O.Ps Posts Divisional M.G. Emplacements and R.A. Work	G.G.J.
	31/1/17		Work continued as above	G.G.J.

1375 Wt. W593/826 1,000,000 4/15 J.B.C. & A. A.D.S.S./Forms/C. 2118.

Secret

Instructions regarding War Diaries and Intelligence Summaries are contained in F. S. Regs., Part II. and the Staff Manual respectively. Title Pages will be prepared in manuscript.

WAR DIARY
or
INTELLIGENCE SUMMARY
(Erase heading not required.)

Army Form C. 2118

513 (London) Field Co. R.E.
(2/2nd London Field Co. R.E.)

Vol 12

Place	Date	Hour	Summary of Events and Information	Remarks and references to Appendices
LAVENTIE	1/3/17		Work continued on Divisional Screen O.P. Posts Divisional M.G. Emplacement and R.A. Work	[initials]
	2/3/17		Further redistribution of RE Company took over old sector from SIGN POST LANE to BOND STREET from 39th Division.	[initials]
HUIT MAISON	3/3/17		Company under command of Captain J. E. VILLA moved from LAVENTIE to HUIT MAISON 2 O.R. rejoined from Hospital	[initials]
	4/3/17		Work continued No 1, 2, & 3 Sections working in front Line & B Line & No 4 Section working in Shops 3 O.R. rejoined from leave	[initials]
	5/3/17		Work continued Major G. T. KINGSFORD proceeded on leave 2 O.R. rejoined from Hospital	[initials]
	[illegible]/3/17		Work continued 2 O.R. proceeded on leave 2 O.R. rejoined from [illegible]	[initials]
	[illegible]/3/17		Work continued 2 O.R. rejoined from Hospital 3 O.R. rejoined from leave	[initials]
	[illegible]/3/17		Work continued	[initials]
	9/3/17		Work continued	[initials]
	10/3/17		Work continued [illegible] on appointment to No 7 Reinforcement RE	[initials]

1875 Wt. W593/826 1,000,000 4/15 J.B.C. & A. A.D.S.S./Forms/C. 2118.

Instructions regarding War Diaries and Intelligence Summaries are contained in F. S. Regs., Part II. and the Staff Manual respectively. Title Pages will be prepared in manuscript.

WAR DIARY
or
INTELLIGENCE SUMMARY
(Erase heading not required.)

Army Form C. 2118

Place	Date	Hour	Summary of Events and Information	Remarks and references to Appendices
[illegible]	11/2/17		Work on tunnel [illegible] Lt F. A. BEIT left for Course of Instruction at R E School [illegible]. [illegible] Lt BEIT	[initials]
	12/2/17		Work continued	[initials]
	13/2/17		" "	[initials]
	14/2/17		Company Rest day. Inspections were carried out & [illegible]	[initials]
	15/2/17		[illegible]	[initials]
	16/2/17		Work continued	[initials]
	17/2/17		Work continued [illegible] O.R. to Hospital	[initials]
	18/2/17		Work continued.	[initials]
	19/2/17		Work continued C.Q.M.S. Foster proceeded to BASE to join No 7 Reinforcement Co RE Authority 1st ARMY No 5768 'A'. 2 O.Rs to Hospital.	[initials]

1875 Wt. W593/826 1,000,000 4/15 J.B.C. & A. A.D.S.S./Forms/C. 2118.

Instructions regarding War Diaries and Intelligence Summaries are contained in F. S. Regs., Part II. and the Staff Manual respectively. Title Pages will be prepared in manuscript.

WAR DIARY
or
INTELLIGENCE SUMMARY
(Erase heading not required.)

Army Form C. 2118

Place	Date	Hour	Summary of Events and Information	Remarks and references to Appendices
HUIT MAISON	20/2/17		Work continued in Front Line. Back Areas & Workshops	J.G.W.
	21/2/17		" "	J.G.W.
	22/2/17		" " 3 O.Rs to Hospital	J.G.W.
	23/2/17		" "	J.G.W.
	24/2/17		" " LT R.O. BEIT & 1 O.R. rejoined Unit from 1st ARMY SCHOOL	J.G.W.
	25/2/17		" " 1 O.R. rejoined from Leave	J.G.W.
	26/2/17		" " MAJOR G.T. KINGSFORD rejoined from Leave	J.G.W.
	27/2/17		Company Rest day Inspections were carried out and Respirator Drill was practised.	J.G.W.
	28/2/17		Work resumed in the Line. The sector between SIGN POST LANE and ~~BOND STREET~~ CHURCH ROAD handed over to 416 Field Co R.E. and new sector from BOND STREET to CANADIAN ORCHARD taken over from 59th Field Co. R.E. No 1 Section relieved No 3 Section on the Left of the new front and No. 2 Section on the Right, No 4 Section in Back Areas and No 3 in Workshops.	J.G.W.

G.T. Kingsford Major R.E.
OC 573 (London) Field Co R.E.

1875 Wt. W593/826 1,000,000 4/15 J.B.C. & A. A.D.S.S./Forms/C. 2118.

Secret

Instructions regarding War Diaries and Intelligence Summaries are contained in F. S. Regs., Part II. and the Staff Manual respectively. Title Pages will be prepared in manuscript.

WAR DIARY
or
INTELLIGENCE SUMMARY
(Erase heading not required.)

Army Form C. 2118

573 (London) Field Coy R.E.

Vol 13

Place	Date	Hour	Summary of Events and Information	Remarks and references to Appendices
HUIT MAISONS	1/3/17		Work continued in Line.	GEW
" "	2/3/17		Work continued in Line	GEW
" "	3/3/17		2/Lt CLIFF proceeded on transfer to Railway Construction Company to ST OMER; work continued in Line - 2/Lieut Macfarlane assumed command of No IV Section in place of 2/Lt CLIFF.	GEW
" "	4/3/17		Work continued in the line - concentration on the reclamation of GUARDS TRENCH so as to complete before handing over.	GEW GEW
" "	5/3/17		1 O.R. to Hospital. Work continued in Line.	GEW
" "	6/3/17		Work continued in the line. 1 O.R. to Hospital. - Work continued in the line.	GEW GEW
" "	7/3/17		1. O.R. to Hospital - Work continued in the line. Lt BEIT returned	GEW
" "	8/3/17		for duty to the company on handing over work to field company of the 49th Division	
" "	9/3/17		Work handed over to 57th Field Company, 49th Division. Company moved to LA GORGUE. Received instructions to proceed to LE COUROY area instead of the WILLEMAN AREA	GEW
LA GORGUE	9/3/17		Company Move from LA GORGUE to ST VENANT AREA (ROBECQ) with column. MAJOR KINGSFORD RE in command of the column	GEW
ROBECQ.	10/3/17		Company move from ROBECQ to VALHOUN with column in command of MAJOR G.T. Kingsford RE	GEW
VALHOUN	11/3/17		1. O.R. to Hospital 1. O.R. from Hospital.	GEW

1875 Wt. W593/826 1,000,000 4/15 J.B.C. & A. A.D.S.S./Forms/C. 2118.

Instructions regarding War Diaries and Intelligence Summaries are contained in F. S. Regs., Part II. and the Staff Manual respectively. Title Pages will be prepared in manuscript.

WAR DIARY
or
~~INTELLIGENCE~~ SUMMARY
(Erase heading not required.)

Army Form C. 2118

Place	Date	Hour	Summary of Events and Information	Remarks and references to Appendices
OPPY.	12/3/17		Company moved from VALHOUN to OPPY in Brigade column under MAJOR KINGSFORD, R.E. under instructions from 168th Bde.	JGW
			1 O.R. returned from leave	
			1 O.R. returned from Hospital	JGW
OPPY.	13/3/17		1 O.R. returned from Hospital	JGW
SIMENCOURT	14/3/17		Company moved to SIMENCOURT under instructions from CRE.	JGW
			Company affiliated to 169th Bde.	
ACHICOURT.	15/3/17		Company ~~to~~ headquarters Transport + Limbers moved to ACHICOURT. Remainder of the Company left at SIMENCOURT under Lt MACFARLANE	JGW
			Work in the line taken over from 89th Field Co R E and 202nd Field Co. RE.	JGW
"	16/3/17		Work on Medium and Heavy Trench Mortar Emplacements commenced	JGW
"	17/3/17		Work on above continued but suspended owing to the evacuation	JGW
"	18/3/17		of Enemy trenches opposite Brigade front.	
"	19/3/17		Work on clearing roads - BEAURAINS-ACHICOURT ROAD and ARRAS-BUCQUOY ROAD making bridges over trenches and strengthening existing bridges.	JGW
"	20/3/17		Work on clearing roads etc continued.	JGW
"	21/3/17		Work on clearing roads etc. continued - 1 O.R. to hospital. - 1 O.R. evacuated.	JGW

1875 Wt. W593/826 1,000,000 4/15 J.B.C. & A. A.D.S.S./Forms/C. 2118.

Instructions regarding War Diaries and Intelligence Summaries are contained in F. S. Regs., Part II. and the Staff Manual respectively. Title Pages will be prepared in manuscript.

WAR DIARY
or
~~INTELLIGENCE SUMMARY~~
(Erase heading not required.)

Army Form C. 2118

Place	Date	Hour	Summary of Events and Information	Remarks and references to Appendices
ACHICOURT	22/3/17		Work on roads and bridges - BEAURAINS - MERCATEL Road. 5 O.R.s from Base. { - BEAURAINS - NEUVILLE VITASSE Road. / Track through NO MANS LAND	J.E.W.
"	23/3/17		Work on roads and bridges handed over to 512 Field Co R.E. - 2 Sections on track through NO MAN'S LAND and 2 Sections at the disposal of 169th Bde working on Brigade Headquarter Dug Out. 1 O.R. to Hospital	J.E.W.
"	24/3/17		Work on Strong Points for 169th Bde (2 Sections) Work on Bde. Headquarter Dug Out Work on cleaning German C.T.'s 2 O.R. to Hospital	J.E.W. J.E.W.
"	25/3/17		Work on Strong Points and Brigade Hq. Dug Out	J.E.W.
"	26/3/17		3 O.R. to Hospital. Work in line - do - do -	J.E.W.
			Work on Strong Points - cleaning German C.T.'s + Hq. Dug-out.	
"	27/3/17		Work on Strong Points and Dug outs for 169th + 168th Bdes	J.E.W.
"	28/3/17		1 O.R. from Hospital.	J.E.W.
"	29/3/17		do. do do do 1. O.R. from Hospital	
"	30/3/17		do. do do. 1 O.R. attached to 416 Field Co R.E. for Sanitary Duties	J.E.W.

C. T. Trinspeard(?)
O.C. 513 FIELD COY. R.E.

1875 Wt. W593/826 1,000,000 4/15 J.B.C. & A. A.D.S.S./Forms/C. 2118.

Secret

Instructions regarding War Diaries and Intelligence Summaries are contained in F. S. Regs., Part II., and the Staff Manual respectively. Title Pages will be prepared in manuscript.

WAR DIARY
or
~~INTELLIGENCE~~ SUMMARY
(Erase heading not required.)

Army Form C. 2118

513 (London) Fd Co RE 56

Vol 14

Place	Date	Hour	Summary of Events and Information	Remarks and references to Appendices
ACHICOURT	1/4/17	-	2 Sections for work under the C.R.E. and 2 Sections under the orders of 167th Brigade – 2 O.R. from Hospital	J.E.W.
"	2/4/17	-	Work on Dug outs. Tramways & Bridges etc	J.E.W.
"	3/4/17	-	do do. do. do. 1 O.R. to Hospital 1. O.R. on Leave.	J.E.W.
"			C.R.E conference at ACHICOURT	J.E.W.
"	4/4/17	-	Work in line as usual – 'V' day of Bombardment.	
"	5/4/17	-	Work in Line as usual – Bombardment postponed one day hence 'V' day bombardment again.	J.E.W.
"	6/4/17	-	Work in line as usual – 'W' day of Bombardment.	J.E.W.
"	7/4/17	-	Work in line as usual – 'X' day of Bombardment – 1 O.R. from Hospital.	J.E.W.
"	8/4/17		Work on Shelters in Ry cutting for Battle Headquarters – Bombardment of Gas Helmets & Box Respirator Drill – Rifle and kit inspections. ACHICOURT Village – 3 O.R's wounded – Y day of Bombardment – HQ & 2 Sections moved to Battle Headquarters	J.E.W.
"	9/4/17		Zero day of Bombardment – 4 Sections on ~~making~~ up roadway – BEAURAINS – MERCATEL Road.	J.E.W.
"	10/4/17		Headquarters returned to billets ACHICOURT. – 4 Sections on work on Roads.	J.E.W.
"	11/4/17		Work on BEAURAINS – MERCATEL Road – 1 O.R transferred to Signal Company.	J.E.W.
"	12/4/17		1. O.R. to Hospital. 2 Sections (Lieut Best and Dain) and Major Kingsford R.E. moved up to NEUVILLE-VITASSE for work under 169th Brigade. – 2 Sections on Roads.	J.E.W.
"	13/4/17		2 Sections on Roads. – 2 Sections away (NEUVILLE-VITASSE.)	J.E.W.

1875 Wt. W593/826 1,000,000 4/15 J.B.C. & A. A.D.S.S./Forms/C. 2118.

Instructions regarding War Diaries and Intelligence Summaries are contained in F. S. Regs., Part II. and the Staff Manual respectively. Title Pages will be prepared in manuscript.

WAR DIARY
or
~~INTELLIGENCE~~ SUMMARY
(Erase heading not required.)

Army Form C. 2118

Place	Date	Hour	Summary of Events and Information	Remarks and references to Appendices
ACHICOURT	14/4/17	–	2 Sections in Forward Area under 168 Bde. orders - on roads. 2 Sections in Back area (ACHICOURT) under C.R.E. - on roads and bridges.	J.E.O.
"	15/4/17	–	Work as above - Gas Helmet instruction, drill and rifle inspection carried out	J.E.O.
"	16/4/17	"	Work as above.	J.E.O.
"	17/4/17	"	Work as above. - Wiring of Strong Point WANCOURT TOWER for L.O.B. - 1 O.R. to Hospital	J.E.O.
"	18/4/17	"	Forward sections withdrawn to ACHICOURT. Warning order to move.	J.E.O.
"	19/4/17	"	Gas Helmet & Box Respirator Drill - Rifle and kit inspection - Loading up of Company vehicles.	J.E.O.
SOUASTRE	20/4/17	"	Company went out to Rest to SOUASTRE AREA with affiliated Brigade (169th) 1 O.R. returned from Leave	J.E.O.
"	21/4/17	"	Complete rest day.	J.E.O.
"	22/4/17	"	Complete rest day with Church Parade in the morning.	J.E.O.
"	23/4/17	"	Training commenced. - Gas Helmet Speed Test - Squad Drill - Cleaning of Company Vehicles - ~~Section~~ Section Equipment overhauled.	J.E.O.
WANQUETIN	24/4/17	"	Training continued. - 1 O.R. from Hospital. - Company Baths. In the afternoon the Company moved with the 169th Brigade to WANQUETIN.	J.E.O.
"	25/4/17	"	Company resting and standing by in billets awaiting further orders Arrival of 5 O.R. from Base as reinforcement to the Company	J.E.O.

1875 Wt. W593/826 1,000,000 4/15 J.B.C. & A. A.D.S.S./Forms/C. 2118.

Instructions regarding War Diaries and Intelligence Summaries are contained in F. S. Regs., Part II. and the Staff Manual respectively. Title Pages will be prepared in manuscript.

WAR DIARY
or
INTELLIGENCE SUMMARY
(Erase heading not required.)

Army Form C. 2118

Place	Date	Hour	Summary of Events and Information	Remarks and references to Appendices
WANQUETIN BERNEVILLE	26.4.17	-	Company moved to BERNEVILLE. Arrival of 2 O.Rs as reinforcement.	JEW
BERNEVILLE	27.4.17.	-	Company resting - 1. O.R. to Hospital. - C.R.E. Operation Order No 95 attached.	JEW
ARRAS.	28/4/17	-	Company moved to ARRAS (in billets) and took over from 91st Field Co R.E.	JEW
"	29/4/17	-	Company on Repairs to Billets - Roads etc	JEW
"	30/4/17	-	Work on Roads in WANCOURT. Road cleared through for R.F.A.	JEW

G. T. [illegible] Major R.E.
O.C. 573 Fd Co R.E.

1875 Wt. W593/826 1,000,000 4/15 J.B.C. & A. A.D.S.S./Forms/C. 2118.

SECRET. Copy No...2...

56th DIVISIONAL ENGINEERS ORDER No. 95.

1. 56th Division is to relieve 15th Division in the Line and has now come under the orders of VI Corps.

2. 416th (Edinburgh) Field Coy R.E. will relieve 73rd Field Coy R.E. on the 28th inst.
Headquarters and Horse Lines will be at G.23.c.5.1.

3. 512th (London) Field Coy R.E. will relieve 74th Field Coy R.E. on the 28th inst.
Headquarters and Horse Lines will be at G.23.c.6.1.

4. 513th (London) Field Coy R.E. will relieve 91st Field Coy R.E. on the 28th inst.
Headquarters will be at G.27.b.8.8., but as the 91st Coy have had Mange in their stables, an Officer will have to be detailed to find convenient Horse Lines.

5. The three Companies will be clear of their present billets by 10 a.m.

6. 1/5th Cheshire Regiment will relieve the Pioneer Battn of the 15th Division on the 28th inst.
Headquarters will be Rue de Rapporteurs, off Théatre Place, G.22.d.1.7. Horse Lines will be at DUISANS.
No restrictions as to route or time.

7. ACKNOWLEDGE.

J.G. Henderson
Capt. & Adjt. R.E.
for C.R.E., 56th Division.

Issued at 3-30 p.m.
27/4/17.

Copy No. 1. 416th (Edinburgh) Field Coy R.E.
2. 512th (London) Field Coy R.E.
3. 513th (London) Field Coy R.E.
4. 1/5th Cheshire Regiment.
5. "G"
6. "Q"
7. 56th Divisional Train.
8. War Diary.
9. File.

Instructions regarding War Diaries and Intelligence Summaries are contained in F. S. Regs., Part II. and the Staff Manual respectively. Title Pages will be prepared in manuscript.

WAR DIARY
or
~~INTELLIGENCE SUMMARY~~
(Erase heading not required.)

Army Form C. 2118

513 Fd Coy R.E.
Vol 15

Place	Date	Hour	Summary of Events and Information	Remarks and references to Appendices
ARRAS.	1.5.17.		Work on Roads - WANCOURT - GUEMAPPE — WANCOURT - MONCHY. - 4 Sections. An enemy aeroplane flying by night dropped a bomb near the Horse Lines (just outside ARRAS) without doing any damage to our Transport. — 2 O.R. wounded at WANCOURT.	J.E.W.
"	2.5.17		The Company attached to C.R.E and in Reserve for the attack on the 3.5.17. Company rest day - Inspection of Rifles - Box Respirator Drill - 1 O.R. to Hospital	J.E.W.
"	3.5.17		Attack commenced at 3.45 am on Diurnal front. - The Company stood by from Zero Hour till dusk that day but owing to the attack being unsuccessful their services were not required that night.	J.E.W.
"	4.5.17		Orders received to relieve the 2 sections of 416 Field Co & 2 Sections of 513 Field Company tomorrow in the line working under 148th Bde. instructions - 2 Sections ordered out urgently by the CRE for Fire duties at ARRAS - Gas alarm sounded. Horses taken ~~away~~ from the Horse Lines to the Race Course. Sections returned at 1.30 am	J.E.W.
"	5.5.17		4 Sections moved up into line - Headquarters & Transport remained in Company billets & Horse Lines ARRAS. The sections were billeted on the WANCOURT - TILLOY Road under Bivouac Shelters & dugouts in the vicinity.	J.E.W.

1875 Wt. W593/826 1,000,000 4/15 J.B.C. & A. A.D.S.S./Forms/C. 2118.

Instructions regarding War Diaries and Intelligence Summaries are contained in F. S. Regs., Part II. and the Staff Manual respectively. Title Pages will be prepared in manuscript.

WAR DIARY
~~or~~
~~INTELLIGENCE SUMMARY~~
(Erase heading not required.)

Army Form C. 2118

Place	Date	Hour	Summary of Events and Information	Remarks and references to Appendices
ARRAS.	6.5.17		4 Sections on Night work digging trenches for the 168th Brigade in the advanced line. Owing to conditions of light etc hostile snipers extremely active - 2 O.R's killed including a Section Sergeant, and 1 O.R. wounded - Enemy barrage on communication trenches heavy.	J.E.W.
"	7.5.17		Company on Strong Point ~~opposite~~ SHRAPNEL TRENCH - Progress good - 1 O.R. to Hospital. Lt R.O. BEIT RE proceeded on transfer to No 9. Army Tramways Co. 2nd Army	J.E.W.
"	8.5.17		Company on Strong Point - 2 O.R.s as reinforcement from Base.	J.E.W.
"	9.5.17		do. - do. 1 O.R from Hospital - 1 O.R. to Hospital.	J.E.W.
"	10.5.17		3 Sections of the Company were relieved by 3 Sections of the 512th Field Co. R.E. and 1 Section was left behind to take part in operations to be carried out on the 11th instant by 168th Brigade. 3 Sections of the 513th Field Company returned to billets in ARRAS (see 56th Divisional Engineer's order No 99) - No 1 Section moved up into ASSEMBLY AREA.	J.E.W.
"	11.5.17		Rest day - gas helmet and rifle inspection. gas helmet drill refitting and kit inspection = No 1 Section spent the whole day in ASSEMBLY AREA - Work to be done - Blocking TOOL TRENCH for 40 yards and putting up a wire entanglement across the trench - 1 O.R. wounded	J.E.W.
"	12.5.17		1 Section under L.O.B relieved by 1 Section 512 Field Co. R.E. 3 Sections under C.R.E. working on the strengthening of the WANCOURT LINE	J.E.W.

1875 Wt. W593/826 1,000,000 4/15 J.B.C. & A. A.D.S.S./Forms/C. 2118.

Instructions regarding War Diaries and Intelligence Summaries are contained in F. S. Regs., Part II. and the Staff Manual respectively. Title Pages will be prepared in manuscript.

WAR DIARY

or

~~INTELLIGENCE SUMMARY~~

(Erase heading not required.)

Army Form C. 2118

Place	Date	Hour	Summary of Events and Information	Remarks and references to Appendices
ARRAS.	12.5.17		WANCOURT LINE – making fire bays and strengthening wire in front of the line No 1 Sect. On being relieved by 512 Field Co. returned to billets ARRAS.	J.E.W.
"	13.5.17		2 Sections on construction of Strong Point – one Section on Divisional Baths at TILLOY and one section on Camping Arrangements for 169th Bde – 1 O.R returned from Hospital.	J.E.W. J.E.W.
"	14.5.17		Work as for the 13th.	J.E.W.
"	15.5.17		4 Sections on Defences of Wancourt. Erection of wire Entanglement from N18 c 1.6 to COJEUL RIVER	J.E.W.
"	16.5.17		do do do do	J.E.W.
"	17.5.17		do do – Warning order of Relief of Division – Company to move to DUISANS.	J.E.W.
"	18.5.17		do do – Arrival of advance party of 152 Field Co (37th Division) who are relieving us	J.E.W.
ARRAS	19.5.17		Company Rest Day – packing of Hq. & Sectional vehicles – Billeting party under sent on ahead under Lieut PINNOCK.	
DUISANS	20.5.17		Billets and Horse Lines handed over to 152 Field Co. RE. The company moved out of ARRAS at 9.15 a.m. – arrival at DUISANS 10.30 a.m	J.E.W.
"	21.5.17		Work on Rifle Ranges construction of Portable Huts for Division – 1 O.R. to Hospl. LT. MACFARLANE proceeded on leave from ARRAS STATION	J.E.W.
"	22.5.17		do do do.	J.E.W.
"	23.5.17		do do do – 2 O.R. to Hospital. MAJOR G.T. KINGSFORD proceeded on leave (AGNEZ-les-DUISANS)	J.E.W.

1875 Wt. W593/826 1,000,000 4/15 J.B.C. & A. A.D.S.S./Forms/C. 2118.

Instructions regarding War Diaries and Intelligence Summaries are contained in F. S. Regs., Part II. and the Staff Manual respectively. Title Pages will be prepared in manuscript.

WAR DIARY
or
INTELLIGENCE SUMMARY
(Erase heading not required.)

Army Form C. 2118

Place	Date	Hour	Summary of Events and Information	Remarks and references to Appendices
GOUVES		24/5/17	Company moved out of DUISANS in Brigade Column at 11.30 a.m. arriving at GOUVES at 12.30 p.m. - work carried on on Ranges. Portable Huts Etc. - 2 O.R's from Hospital	J.E.W.
GOUVES		25/5/17	Assistance to Brigade in Improvement to Billeting arrangements - Construction of Model Fire Trench (new pattern) for G.O.C's inspection - Model of Cruciform Strong Point commenced for Training Purposes - Lt SMAIL proceeded on transfer to 283rd Army Troops Company.	J.E.W. J.E.W.
"		26/5/17	Inspection of Fire Trench dug by the company by General HULL; G.O.C 56th Division. Work as above.	J.E.W.
"		27/5/17	Work as above - 4 O.R's as reinforcement from the Base. Training commenced. Trestle & Pontoon Bridging and work in hand in course of completion	J.E.W.
"		28/5/17	Training continued as above - work on Strong Point - Report made to A.D.V.S through V.O. attached 169th Bde on improper burial of horses near Company Lines - He found out they belonged to the 29th Div. Art'y.	J.E.W.
"		29/5/17		
"		30.5.17	Training continued - work on Strong Point - 1 O.R. to Hospital - Warning Order for move received from CRE.	J.E.W.
"		31.5.17	Company Rest Day - Rifle and Gas Helmet Inspection - 3 officers to ARRAS to take over work in the line - 4 O.R's to Hospital	J.E.W.

[signature] Capt. R.E.
for O.C. 513 Field Co.

Instructions regarding War Diaries and Intelligence Summaries are contained in F. S. Regs., Part II. and the Staff Manual respectively. Title Pages will be prepared in manuscript.

WAR DIARY
or
~~INTELLIGENCE SUMMARY~~
(Erase heading not required.)

Army Form C. 2118

513th (London) Field Coy R E

Vol 16

Place	Date	Hour	Summary of Events and Information	Remarks and references to Appendices
ARRAS - TILLOY	1.6.17		Company left billets at GOUVES at 10.0 am and proceeded to ARRAS where CQMS Stores, HQ and Horse Lines were left under charge of 2/Lt BOURNE – 4 Sections and HQ Clerical Staff proceeded to forward area and bivouacked in the wood just outside TILLOY VILLAGE – 1 O.R. to Hospital	JEW
"	2.6.17		Work commenced on Mine Dug Outs for 37th & 29th DIVARTY. – 1 O.R to Hospital	JEW
"	3.6.17		Work as above – 2 O.R's to Hospital	JEW
"	4.6.17		Work as above – 5 O.R's reinforcement from the Base	JEW
"	5.6.17		Work as above – 1 O.R to Hospital	JEW
"	6.6.17		Work as above – 1 O.R. reinforcement from ~~Hospital~~ Base – Warning Order for Div to move into line received – MAJOR G.T. Kingsford returned from Leave (7.6.17)	JEW
"	7.6.17		Work as above – 2/Lt MACFARLANE returned from Leave – 2 O.R's to Hospital	JEW
"	8.6.17		Work as above	
"	9.6.17		Work as above – 2/Lt DAIN proceeded on leave – 2 O.R's from Hospital – 1 OR to Hospital	JEW
"	10.6.17		Work as above – 1 OR reinforcement from Base	
"	11.6.17		Work on Mine Dug Outs for Artillery handed over to 476th Field Co RE 61st Div. Rest day for Company – Rifle and Gas Helmet inspection – 1 OR from Hospital – 10 OR's reinforcement from Base	JEW
"	12.6.17		Company Training – Section Drill etc in the morning – afternoon off – 2 OR's to Hospital	JEW

1875 Wt. W593/826 1,000,000 4/15 J.B.C. & A. A.D.S.S./Forms/C. 2118.

Instructions regarding War Diaries and Intelligence Summaries are contained in F. S. Regs., Part II. and the Staff Manual respectively. Title Pages will be prepared in manuscript.

WAR DIARY
or
~~INTELLIGENCE~~ SUMMARY
(Erase heading not required.)

Army Form C. 2118

Place	Date	Hour	Summary of Events and Information	Remarks and references to Appendices
ARRAS TILLOY	13.6.17		1 Section on Erection of Shelters for 167th Bde - 2 Sections on Mine Dug Outs in Forward Area for 169th Bde and 1 Section on work in ARRAS	JEW
"	14.6.17		2 O.R. from Hospital - work as above	JEW
"	15.6.17		work as above 1 O.R. from Hospital - 1 O.R. to Hospital. 5 OR's reinforcement.	JEW
"	16.6.17		work as above -	JEW
"	17.6.17		work as above - 2 ORs to Hospital.	JEW
"	18.6.17		Work as above -	JEW
"	19.6.17		work as above - 5-O.R's reinforcement from the Base.	JEW
"	20.6.17		work as above. - Rifle and Gas helmet inspection for Sections 3 & 4 owing to 3 shifts being knocked off for the day through lack of material	JEW
"	21.6.17		work as above - 1 O.R. on leave.	
"	22.6.17		work as above on Mine Dug Outs etc. 2/Lt DAIN returned from leave	GJK
"	23.6.17		work as above.	GJK
"	24.6.17		work as above - 1. O.R. to Hospital	GJK
"	25.6.17		work as above. - 1. O.R. to Hospital.	GJK
"	26.6.17		work as above. Lt Bowen left unit on 10 days leave	GJK
"	27.6.17		work as above - Warning Order from C.R.E for 2 Sections to proceed to GRAND RULLECOURT to put up bayonet fighting gallows etc.	GJK
"	28.6.17		H.Q. & Nos 1 & 2 Sections under command of Capt Villa R.E. proceeded to Grand Rullecourt for work in back area - 1. OR to hospital 1. OR from Hospital. Work on dugouts completed	GJK

Instructions regarding War Diaries and Intelligence Summaries are contained in F. S. Regs., Part II. and the Staff Manual respectively. Title Pages will be prepared in manuscript.

WAR DIARY
or
~~INTELLIGENCE SUMMARY~~
(Erase heading not required.)

Army Form C. 2118

Place	Date	Hour	Summary of Events and Information	Remarks and references to Appendices
Tilloy	29/6/17	-	Work continued on "T" heads & wiring of communication trenches. 1 OR rejoined from leave. HQ + 2 sections at GRAND RULLECOURT	GIK
"	30/6/17		Work completed as above.	GIK
			G. T. Mungford Major RE OC 573 Fd Coy RE	

1875 Wt. W593/826 1,000,000 4/15 J.B.C. & A. A.D.S.S./Forms/C. 2118.

(in pads of 100).

MESSAGES AND SIGNALS.

No. of Message ....

Prefix .... Code .... m.	Words	Charge	This message is on a/c of:	Recd. at .... m.
Office of Origin and Service Instructions.	Sent		.... Service.	Date ....
	At .... m.			From ....
	To			
	By		(Signature of "Franking Officer.")	By ....

TO CRE

Sender's Number.	Day of Month.	In reply to Number.	AAA
* S 5/8	4/6/17		

I enclose herewith War Diary for May AAA It is regretted that this was not sent in before please.

Firth
Capt R.E.
for O.C. 513 (London) Field Coy R.E.

513TH
(LONDON) FIELD COY.,
R.E.
No. ....
Date 4/6/17.

From
Place
Time

The above may be forwarded as now corrected. (Z)

.... Censor. Signature of Addressor or person authorised to telegraph in his name.

* This line should be erased if not required.

750,000. W 2186—M509. H. W. & V., Ld. 6/16.

57 Horrocs. W D
136 men.

SECRET. Copy No.......

56th Divisional Engineers Order No. 104.

1. The 513th (London) Field Coy R.E. (less two sections) will move to GRAND RULLECOURT on the 28th instant.

2. Rations for 48 hours will be carried.

Ration indent for 30th instant will be handed to Town Major, AVESNES LE COMTE AS THE Company passes through there, and arrangements made with him for drawing the rations.

3. No restrictions as to route, but Company will arrive at GRAND RULLECOURT by 3 p.m. in order to offload two lorry loads of stores which are being delivered there.

4. Billets will be allotted by the Billet Warden, GRAND RULLECOURT.

Issued at 4-15 p.m.
27th June 1917.

J. J. Henderson
Capt. & Adjt. R.E.
for C.R.E., 56th Division.

Copy No. 1. 513th (London) Field Coy R.E.
2. "G"
3. "Q"
4. War Diary.
5. File.

Secret

Instructions regarding War Diaries and Intelligence Summaries are contained in F. S. Regs., Part II. and the Staff Manual respectively. Title Pages will be prepared in manuscript.

WAR DIARY
or
~~INTELLIGENCE SUMMARY~~
(Erase heading not required.)

573 (London) Fd Coy R.E.

Army Form C. 2118

Vol. 17

Place	Date	Hour	Summary of Events and Information	Remarks and references to Appendices
TILLOY & GRAND RULLECOURT	1/7/17		Two Sections (1&2) and HQ at GRAND RULLECOURT on work for the Division - Construction of Targets Rifle Ranges, Assault Courses etc. - Two Sections (3&4) at TILLOY completing work in the line - Mined Dug-Outs, 'T' Heads etc	JEO
"	2/7/17		do do do do	JEO
GOUY & GRAND RULLECOURT	3/7/17		Two Sections ~~at~~ at TILLOY moved to GOUY-en-ARTOIS - 1 O.R. to Hospital. The other two Sections completing work on Rifle Ranges etc.	JEO
SOMBRIN	4/7/17		HQ and 2 Sections moved to SOMBRIN and the two Sections at GOUY moved to SOMBRIN.	JEO
"	5/7/17		Company rest day. - 1 O.R. from Hospital - 1 O.R. from Leave	JEO
"	6/7/17		do. do. do. - Brigade Rehearsal of Ceremonial Church Parade. 1 OR from Base Depot	
"	7/7/17		Company Rehearsal for Ceremonial Church Parade in the morning - Company drill and cleaning up parade. - 9 O.Rs to 3rd Army Rest Camp.	JEO
"	8/7/17		Ceremonial Church Parade postponed owing to weather - Company Drill	JEO
"	9/7/17		Training commenced. - Wiring Drill etc. etc. Major Kingsford R.E. acting C.R.E.	JEO
"	10/7/17		Training continued. - CAPT VILLA proceeded on Leave 2. O.Rs from Hospital	GIK
"	11/7/17		Training continued - 1 O.R. from Base Depot	GIK
"	12/7/17		Training continued - 2 O.Rs to Hospital	GIK
"	13/7/17		Training continued.	GIK
"	14/7/17		Training continued.	GIK

1875 Wt. W593/826 1,000,000 4/15 J.B.C. & A. A.D.S.S./Forms/C. 2118.

Army Form C. 2118

Instructions regarding War Diaries and Intelligence Summaries are contained in F. S. Regs., Part II. and the Staff Manual respectively. Title Pages will be prepared in manuscript.

WAR DIARY
or
~~INTELLIGENCE SUMMARY~~
(Erase heading not required.)

Place	Date	Hour	Summary of Events and Information	Remarks and references to Appendices
SOMERIN	15/7/17		Training continued in the morning - 1 O.R from Hospital. In the afternoon R.E. Sports took place.	GIK
"	16/7/17		Training continued - 1. O.R to Hospital - 1. O.R. Leave to U.K.	GIK
"	17/7/17		69th Brigade Horse Show, & Sports in which the Company took part. Training continued - 3. O.Rs to Hospital. Brigade Sports.	GIK
"	18/7/17		Training continued	GIK
"	19/7/17		Training continued - 2/Lt PINNOCK proceeded on Leave to U.K.	GIK
"	20/7/17		Training continued } 2 O.Rs to Hospital }	GIK
"	21/7/17		Packing Parade & cleaning up billets.	GIK
BOUQUE-MAISON	22/7/17		Company marched to BOUQUEMAISON & stayed the night there.	
HALLINES	23/7/17		Company entrained at BOUQUEMAISON and proceeded by rail to WIZERNES detrained and marched to HALLINES where they stayed the night.	GIK
WESTROVE	24/7/17		Company marched from HALLINES to WESTROVE with 2nd LONDON Regt	GIK
"	25/7/17		Rifle, Gas Helmet, Kit, and ~~Foot~~ Inspections - CAPT VILLA returned from Leave.	
"	26/7/17		Company Training - one section on works under CRE Corps Troops V Corps	JW
"	27/7/17		Company Training - do do do.	JW

1875 Wt. W593/826 1,000,000 4/15 J.B.C. & A. A.D.S.S./Forms/C. 2118.

Army Form C. 2118

Instructions regarding War Diaries and Intelligence Summaries are contained in F. S. Regs., Part II. and the Staff Manual respectively. Title Pages will be prepared in manuscript.

WAR DIARY
or
~~INTELLIGENCE SUMMARY~~
(Erase heading not required.)

Place	Date	Hour	Summary of Events and Information	Remarks and references to Appendices
WESTROVE	28/7/17		Company Training – one Section on works under C.R.E Corps Troops V Corps	JEW
"	29/7/17		do – do do – do –	JEW
"	30/7/17		do – do – do – do –	JEW
"	31/7/17		do – do – do – do – Lt PINNOCK RE ~~proceeded~~ returned from Leave	JEW

G. T. [illegible] Major RE
O.C. 573 Fd Co RE

1875 Wt. W593/826 1,000,000 4/15 J.B.C. & A. A.D.S.S./Forms/C. 2118.

Instructions regarding War Diaries and Intelligence Summaries are contained in F. S. Regs., Part II. and the Staff Manual respectively. Title Pages will be prepared in manuscript.

WAR DIARY

or

~~INTELLIGENCE SUMMARY~~

(Erase heading not required.)

Army Form C. 2118

573 Fd Coy RE

Vol 18

Place	Date	Hour	Summary of Events and Information	Remarks and references to Appendices
WESTROVE	1st Aug.		General Training including Lectures. Work hampered by bad weather.	JEW
"	2nd "		do do. do. do. do 1. OR. ~~went~~ on Leave	JEW
"	3rd "		do do - Pontooning on Lake at HOULLE. Warning Order for move received. 1 OR to Hospital	JEW
"	4th "		Packing of Pontoon Wagons and Stores. - Orders for Move received at 11.0 pm	JEW
NORDPREENE	5th "		Move from WESTROVE to NORDPREENE with 169th Brigade Transport and a portion of Divisional Transport under command of Major G.T. Kingsford RE. Left ~~NORDPREENE~~ WESTROVE at 3.0 am and arrived NORDPREENE at 1.0 P.M. - Halt outside ST OMER for an hour and a quarter.	JEW
WIPPENHOEK	6th "		Moved from NORDPREENE to WIPPENHOEK under command of Major Kingsford RE. Left NORDPREENE at 7.0 am and arrived WIPPENHOEK at 1.30 P.M. - Company billeted in tents and shelters.	JEW
"	7th		Rifle, Gas Helmet and Box Respirator Inspection. 2 OR.s to Hospital, 1 O.R. from Hospital	JEW
"	8th		Drill in Box Respirators and Improvements to Sanitation etc in Camp.	JEW
"	9th		Work under C.E. IInd Corps - 4 Sections - 1 OR from Hospital	JEO
"	10th		do do. Lt. Bourne to Hospital	JEO
CHATEAU SEGARD.	11		do do 2 OR's to Hosp. 1 O.R. rejoined from Leave - Lt Palmer attached RE admitted sick to hospital - Orders received to proceed up the Line - Arrived CHATEAU SEGARD 9.30 PM	JEO
"	12th		Construction of Camp ~~at~~ CHATEAU SEGARD - 1. OR. proceeded on leave.	JEO
"	13th		Construction of Strong Point J.14 a.2.2 on the night 13/14th.	JEO
"	14th		Work on Dug outs for Bde. - 1. OR killed and 1. O R. wounded.	JEO

1875 Wt. W593/826 1,000,000 4/15 J.B.C. & A. A.D.S.S./Forms/C. 2118.

Instructions regarding War Diaries and Intelligence Summaries are contained in F. S. Regs., Part II. and the Staff Manual respectively. Title Pages will be prepared in manuscript.

WAR DIARY
or
~~INTELLIGENCE SUMMARY~~

(Erase heading not required.)

Army Form C. 2118

Place	Date	Hour	Summary of Events and Information	Remarks and references to Appendices
CHATEAU SEGARD	15th		4 Sections under 169th Bde moved to forward Battle area to stand by for work on the morning of 16th (See Bde Operation Order No. 111). – 2 O.R's to Hospital	[initials]
"	~~16th~~		One party under 2/Lt MACFARLANE successfully carried out "taping" of "forming-up" line for 169th Bde.	
"	16th		Operations commenced, Zero Hour 4.45 a.m. – Company stood by the whole day at Bde. HQ. – work on wiring original front line on the night of the 16/17th	[initials]
"	17th		4 Sections returned to CHATEAU-SEGARD – Warning order received from C.R.E. for a move at short notice – 1 O.R. to Hospital	[initials]
WIPPENHOEK	18th		Work handed over to 61st Field Co RE 14th Division – 1 officer left behind to show relieving company round the line. Dismounted Personnel proceeded by Busses to WIPPENHOEK and transport by road to the same place.	[initials]
"	19th		Rifle Inspection and Box Respirator Drill – 3 O.R. to Hospital.	[initials] [initials]
"	20th		Training commenced. – 3 O.R. to Hospital	
"	21st		do 3 O.R.s from Hospital, 1 O.R. rejoined from Base, 1 O.R. to Hospital 1. O.R. proceeded on leave.	[initials]
"	22nd		Training – 1 O.R. proceeded on leave – Warning order for move received.	[initials]
"	23rd		Dismounted Personnel remained at WIPPENHOEK. Transport proceeded by road to ARNEKE – 1 O.R. from Hospital.	[initials]
"	24th		Dismounted Personnel proceeded by train from ABEELE Station to WATTEN Station, and transport ~~moved~~ from ARNEKE	[initials]

1875 Wt. W593/826 1,000,000 4/15 J.B.C. & A. A.D.S.S./Forms/C. 2118.

Instructions regarding War Diaries and Intelligence Summaries are contained in F. S. Regs., Part II. and the Staff Manual respectively. Title Pages will be prepared in manuscript.

WAR DIARY
or
~~INTELLIGENCE SUMMARY~~
(Erase heading not required.)

Army Form C. 2118

Place	Date	Hour	Summary of Events and Information	Remarks and references to Appendices
WESTROVE	24th		ARNEKE area to WESTROVE. On arrival at WATTEN the dismounted personnel proceeded by road to WESTROVE – 1 O.R. to Hospital – 1. O.R. from leave.	J.E.W.
"	25th		Company Parade, censorship rules read out to the men by O.C. – Rifle Kit, and Gas Helmet Inspection – Box Respirator Drill.	J.E.W.
"	26th		Company Rest Day.	J.E.W.
"	27th		Company Training	J.E.W.
"	28th		Company Training – Warning order for move received – Pontoons brought back from HOULLE	J.E.W.
"	29th		Arrangements for move made	J.E.W.
WIZERNES	30th		Company marched to WIZERNES Station where they entrained in strategical train. Arrival at WIZERNES Station 12.45 pm departure 3.54 Pm – Detrained at 1.0 am on 31st August – ~~at~~ MIRAUMONT Stn and marched to camp on BAPAUME – BANCOURT ROAD – Company billeted in tents.	J.E.W.
BAPAUME BANCOURT ROAD CAMP	31st			J.E.W.
	1st Sep			

J E Wella Capt RE
for O.C. 513 Field Co

1875 Wt. W593/826 1,000,000 4/15 J.B.C. & A. A.D.S.S./Forms/C. 2118.

SECRET.

Copy No...17.

169TH INFANTRY BRIGADE ORDER No. 107.

****

Reference.
HAZEBROUCK 5A.
1/100,000.

4th Aug. 1917.

1. The 56th Division (less Artillery) will be transferred from 5th Corps to II Corps by road and rail. Moves by road on the 5th August will be in accordance with attached March Table.

2. Entraining Stations will be WATTEN and ST. OMER. Instructions as to moves by rail will be issued later.

3. The column moving by road will be under the immediate Command of Major KINGSFORD, R.E. The 169th Infantry Brigade Group will consist on the 5th instant of the Units shown on March Table.

4. (a) On the 6th instant the 169th Infantry Brigade Group will move under orders to be issued by Major KINGSFORD to the WIPPENHOEK Area (L.28 and 34. Map Sheet 27.).

(b) Route via CASSEL and STEENVORDE. To march at 7 a.m. March to be completed by 12 noon. Billets from Area Commandant WIPPENHOEK (L.21.c.4.4. Map Sheet 27).

(c) For this move the 169th Brigade Group will consist of

Units of the 169th Infantry Brigade.
513th Field Coy. R.E.
2/3rd Ldn. Field Ambulance.
No. 4 Coy. Divisional Train.
1/5th Cheshire Regt.
193rd M.G.Coy. on 5th inst

5. (a) Billeting parties for the Road Portion will proceed in advance reporting to Area Commandant at NOORDPEENE as early as possible.

(b) Usual certificates must be rendered to this office to the effect that areas are left in a clean and sanitary condition.

(c) All claims must be settled before leaving, an Officer being left behind to obtain the certificate from the Mayor that there are no claims against the Troops in addition to those which have already been submitted.

6. ACKNOWLEDGE.

L. Carden Roe.
Capt.
Bde. Major. 169th Inf. Bde.

Issued at midnight

COPIES
1 - 3 Staff.
4 War Diary.
5 2nd Londons.
6. L.R.B.
7 Q.V.R.
8 Q.W.R.
9 169th M.G.Coy.
10 169th T.M.B.
11 56th Divn. G.
12 C.R.E.
13. 56th Divn. Signals.
14. 56th Divn. Train.
15. 193rd M.G.Coy.
16. 1/5th Cheshires.
17. 513th Field Coy. R.E.
18. Major KINGSFORD.
19. 2/3rd Field Ambulance.
20. No. 4 Coy. Divn. Train.
21. Officer i/c Signals.
22. Bde. Transport Officer.

MARCH TABLE to accompany 169TH INFANTRY BRIGADE ORDER No.107.

Serial Number.	Order of March.	Starting Point	Time to pass S.P.	Route.	Destination	Remarks.
No. 1.	Divnl.R.E. H.Q.	Road junction immediately S.W. of the H in MOULLE.	4. 5 am.	ST. OMER - CLAIRMAIRAIS.	NORDPEENE	Units must not turn in on to the Main NORDAUSQUES - ST. OMER Road until the unit due to precede them at the S.P. has passed. (This applies to Serial Numbers 3, 7, 11, 12, 14.
2	Divnl.Signal Coy.		4. 6 am.			
3	Divnl. Train		4. 7 am.			
4	193rd M.G.Coy.		4. 9 am.			
5	1/5th Cheshires.		4.11 am.			
6	169th Bde. H.Q.		4.14 am.			
7	L.R.B.		4.15 am.			
8	Q.W.R.		4.18 am.			
9	Q.V.R.		4.21 am.			
10	2nd Londons.		4.24 am.			
11	169th M.G.Coy.		4.27 am.			
12	No.4 Coy. Divnl. Train.		4.29 am.			
13	513th Field Coy. R.E.		4.31 am.			
14	2/3rd London Field Ambulance.		4.34 am.			

N.B. March to be completed by 10 a.m.

SECRET. Copy No....2.....

56th Divisional Engineers Order No. 108.

1. The 56th Division will on the night 12th/13th August relieve the 18th and 25th Divisions on the front between the SURBITON VILLAS - BLACK WATCH CORNER Road (inclusive to 56th Division) and the WESTHOEK - ZONNEBEKE Road (inclusive to 25th Division), in accordance with instructions which are being issued separately.

2. 416th (Edinburgh) Field Coy R.E. and 513th (London) Field Coy R.E. will move this afternoon to CHATEAU SEGARD.

3. No restrictions as to time or route.

4. Advance party will report to Area Commandant, CHATEAU SEGARD, H.30.a.2.8.

5. Location of Transport Lines will follow.

6. Intervals of 200 yards between Coys and 500 yards between Battns will be maintained on the march.

7. ACKNOWLEDGE.

Issued at 11-30 a.m.
11/8/17.

J H Gordon
Lieut. Colonel R.E.
C.R.E., 56th Division.

Copy No. 1. 512th (London) Field Coy R.E.
2. 513th (London) Field Coy R.E.
3. 416th (Edinburgh) Field Coy R.E.
4. "G"
5. War Diary.
6. File.

SECRET. Copy No...2...

56th Divisional Engineers Order No. 110.

1. The 56th Division will, on the night 12th/13th August relieve the portions of 18th and 25th Divisions on the front between the SURBITON VILLAS - BLACK WATCH CORNER Road (inclusive to 56th Division) and the WESTHOEK - ZONNEBEKE Road (inclusive to 25th Division).

2. The 53rd Infantry Brigade and attached troops of 18th Division will come under the Command of G.O.C., 56th Division from 10 a.m. 13th August.

3. ~~MXMXM~~ 169th Infantry Brigade will relieve 53rd Infantry Bde (18th Division), H.Q. DORMY HOUSE, on the front between the SURBITON VILLAS - BLACK WATCH CORNER Road (inclusive to 169th Brigade) and the road running from HOOGE CHATEAU along the Northern edge of GLENCORSE WOOD (inclusive to 167th Infantry Brigade) H.Q. of 169th Brigade - HALFWAY HOUSE.

4. 167th Infantry Brigade will relieve 75th Infantry Brigade (25th Division) H.Q. BIRR cross roads, on the front from the last named road (inclusive) to the WESTHOEK - ZONNEBEKE Road (exclusive) H.Q. of 167th Infantry Brigade - HALFWAY HOUSE.

5. Boundaries will be as follows :-

Between 56th Division and 25th Division on left (or 8th Divn. when this relieves the 25th Division) :-
Cross Roads WESTHOEK STN. - I.18.b.1.6. (HOOGE) - thence I.16.d.6.5. (HALFWAY HOUSE inclusive).

Between 56th Division and 24th Division on right.
Existing boundary between 18th and 24th Divisions, i.e., J.19.b.95.85. - GREEN JACKET RIDGE - OBSERVATORY RIDGE Road - Road junction S. of ZILLEBEKE.

Between 53rd Infantry Brigade and 169th Infantry Brigade.
BLACK WATCH CORNER - SURBITON VILLAS Road (inclusive to 169th Brigade) - J.13.c.9.2. - J.19.a.1.4. - S. end of MAPIE COPSE.

Between 169th Infantry Brigade and 167th Infantry Brigade.
Cross roads J.7.d. - J.13.a.7.3. - J.13.c.3.8. - J.18.d.5.2. - thence YEOMANRY POST inclusive.

The AREA within the Divisional Boundaries WEST of a line running N. & S. through ZILLEBEKE is common to the three Brigades.

6. Accommodation in HALFWAY HOUSE & RITZ dugouts will be equally shared between 167th & 169th Infantry Brigades.

7. All arrangements for relief of Field Coys will be made by the C.R.E. direct.

8. Work in hand, dumps, air photos, maps, etc. will be taken over by all concerned.

9. The Command of the Divisional Sector will be assumed by G.O.C. 56th Division at 10 a.m., 13th inst.

10. 56th Divn. R.E. H.Q. will close at RENINGHELST at 8 a.m. and will open at H.27.b.5.7. at 10 a.m. on 13th instant.

Issued at 4 p.m.
12/8/17.

Capt. & Adjt. R.E.
for C.R.E., 56th Division.

Copy No. 1. 512th (London) Field Coy R.E.
2. 513th (London) Field Coy R.E.
3. 416th (Edinburgh) Field Coy R.E.
4. "G"
5. "Q"
6. War Diary.
7. File.

SECRET.   Copy No....2........

56th DIVISIONAL ENGINEERS' ORDER No. 116.

1. 14th Division will relieve 56th Division (less Artillery) and 53rd Infantry Brigade (attached) on the night 17th/18th. inst.

2. Movements in relief will take place in accordance with attached March Table. Intervals of 200 yards between Companies and 500 yards between Battalions will be maintained on the march.

3. Maps, photos, Intelligence Notes, etc. will be handed over to relieving units.

4. Command of the front will be taken over by G.O.C., 14th Division at 10 a.m. on 18th August, 1917.

5. One Officer of 513th and 416th Field Companies and one Officer of 1/5th. Cheshires will remain behind one day to act as guides to the relieving units.

6. 56th. Divisional Engineers' H.Q. will close at H.27.b.6.8. at 9 a.m. on 18th inst. and open at RENINGHELST at 11 a.m.

7. ACKNOWLEDGE. ✓

Issued at 10-45 p.m.
on 17/8/17.

Capt. & Adjt. R.E.,
for C.R.E., 56th. Division.

Copy No. 1 512th Field Co. R.E.
✓2. 513th Field Co. R.E.
3 416th Field Co. R.E.
4 "G"
5 "Q"
6 War Diary.
7 File.

MARCH TABLE TO ACCOMPANY 56th DIVISIONAL ENGINEERS' ORDER No. 116.

Serial No.	Date.	Unit.	From	To	Remarks.
1.	Aug. 18th.	167 Inf Bde (less 3 Bns.) 416th Field Coy.	CHATEAU SEGRAD.	STEENVOORDE EAST.	Embus DICKEBUSCH - CAFE BELGE Road. Tail of Column at CAFE BELGE. Column moves off 8-15 a.m. Billets from Area Commandant, STEENVOORDE.
2.	" 18th.	169 Inf Bde (less 2 Bns.) 513th Field Coy.	-do-	WIPPENHOEK Area.	By lorry from CAFE BELGE at 11 a.m. Tail of Column at CAFE BELGE. Billets from Area Commandant, WIPPENHOEK L.21.c.4.4. (Sheet 27)
3.	" 18th.	512th Field Coy.	-do-	OTTAWA CAMP.	No restrictions as to time or route.
4.	" 18th.	Transport of Serial No. 1.	Present Camp.	STEENVOORDE EAST.	Via RENINGHELST - ABEELE. To enter ABEELE at 9-30a.m.
5.	" 18th.	Transport of Serial No. 2.	-do-	WIPPENHOEK Area.	Move off immediately in rear of Serial No. 2., via RENINGHELST.

SECRET. Copy No...2.....

56th DIVISIONAL ENGINEERS' ORDER No. 117.

Ref. Map 1/100,000 HAZEBROUCK.

1. 56th Division (less Artillery & Pioneer Battalion) will move from 11 Corps Area to V Corps Area (EPERLECQUES) in accordance with the attached March Table.

2. Mounted portions of Division halting for the night at NOORDPEENE will report in advance to the Area Commandant, NOORDPEENE, for details as to accommodation.

3. 512th (London) Field Co. R.E. will move in accordance with the attached March Table.
513th (London) Field Co. R.E. will move under orders of G.O.C., 169th Infantry Brigade.
416th (Edinburgh) Field Co. R.E. will move under orders of G.O.C., 167th Infantry Brigade.

4. The following intervals will be maintained on the march:-

(a) East of RENINGHELST - POPERINGHE Road - 200 yds. between Companies.

(b) West of above road - 500 yards between Battalions.

5. Div. R.E. H.Q. will close at RENINGHELST at 9 a.m. 24th August, and open at EPERLECQUES at 11 a.m. on same day.

6. ACKNOWLEDGE.

Issued at 3 p.m. on 22/8/17.

J.J. Henderson
Capt. & Adjt., R.E., for C.R.E., 56th Division.

Copy No. 1 512th Field Co. R.E.
2 513th Field Co. R.E.
3 416th Field Co. R.E.
4 "G"
5 "Q"
6 War Diary.
7 File.

MARCH TABLE TO ACCOMPANY 56th DIVISIONAL ENGINEERS' ORDER No. 117.

Serial No.	Date	Unit.	From	To	Remarks.
1.	Aug. 22nd.	Mounted portion of 167th Inf.Bde.Group.	STEENVOORDE E. Area	NOORDPEENE Area.	Via OUDEZEELE & HARDIFORT. To be clear of STEENVOORDE by 4 p.m.
2.	23rd.	-do-	NOORDPEENE Area	EPERLECQUES Area (GANSPETTE)	Via LEDERZEELE - WATTEN - GANSPETTE. March to be completed by 10 a.m.
3.	23rd.	167th Inf.Bde.Group. (less Mounted portion)	STEENVOORDE E. Area.	EPERLECQUES Area (GANSPETTE)	By train. Entraining Station & hour to be notified by "Q" 56th Divn.
4.	23rd.	Mounted portion of 169th Inf.Bde.Group.	WIPPENHOEK Area.	NOORDPEENE Area.	Via STEENVOORDE - OUDEZEELE - HARDIFORT. Head of column to enter ARNEKE at 2-30pm.
5.	23rd.	Mounted portion of 168th Inf.Bde.Group.	OUDERDOM & RENINGHELST.	-do-	To follow Serial No. 4. Head of column to enter ARNEKE at 2-30 p.m.
6.	24th.	Serial No. 4.	NOORDPEENE Area.	SERQUES Area.	Via CLAIRMARAIS - ST OMER - TILQUES - MONNECOVE. To enter TILQUES at 8 a.m.
7.	24th.	Serial No. 5.	-do-	HOULLE Area.	To follow Serial No.6. To enter TILQUES at 9 a.m.
8.	24th.	Dismounted portions of Serial Nos. 4 & 5.	WIPPENHOEK - OUDERDOM & RENINGHELST.	SERQUES, HOULLE & EPERLECQUES Area.	By train. Entraining Station & times to be notified by 56th Div. "Q"
9.	25th.	Mounted portion of 513th Field Co. R.E.	BUSSEBOOM.	NOORDPEENE Area.	Via ABEELE-STEENVOORDE-OUDEZEELE & HARDIFORT. Head of column to enter ARNEKE at 2-30 p.m.

Continued.

Serial No.	Date.	Unit.	From	To.	Remarks.
10.	Aug. 26th.	Serial No. 9.	NOORDPEENE Area.	HOULLE Area.	Via CLAIRMARAIS - ST OMER - TILQUES. No restrictions as to time.
11.	26th.	Dismounted portion of 512th Field Co. R.E.	BUSSEBOOM.	-do-	By bus or train - details to be notified by "Q", 56th. Division.

Instructions regarding War Diaries and Intelligence Summaries are contained in F. S. Regs., Part II. and the Staff Manual respectively. Title Pages will be prepared in manuscript.

WAR DIARY
or
~~INTELLIGENCE SUMMARY~~
(Erase heading not required.)

Army Form C. 2118

513 Fd Coy R.E.

Vol 19

Place	Date	Hour	Summary of Events and Information	Remarks and references to Appendices
BAPAUME — BANCOURT Rd CAMP.	1st Sept		Erection & Screening of latrines for 169th Bde. – Work at Divisional H.Q. – ~~1 O.R. to Hospital~~	J.E.W.
"	2nd "		Company Rest Day. Box Respirator Inspection & Drill. 1 O.R. to Hospital – 4 Sections Sappers moved to ROCQUINY for work on Rifle Range for Corps.	R.E.W.
"	3rd "		Work on Rifle Range – 3 O.R.s reinforcement from Base –	J.E.W.
"	4th "		Warning order for move to the line received – 1 O.R. from Leave, 1 O.R. on Leave to U.K. – 1 O.R. from Hospital.	J.E.W.
LEBUQUIERE	5th "		Company (less Sappers) moved from BANCOURT CAMP to LEBUQUIERE – Sappers marched direct from ROCQUIGNY to LEBUCQUIERE – 1 O.R. from Leave – 1 O.R. to Hospital	J.E.W.
"	6th "		Improvements to Camp – construction of Horse Standings – 2 O.Rs to Hospital	J.E.W.
"	7th "		do do. Work in Line. Construction of Deep Dug outs – Repairs to Baths – erection of Winter Hutting – 1 O.R. to Hospital, 2 O.Rs on Leave	J.E.W.
"	8th "		Work as above – 2 O.Rs on Leave.	J.E.W.
"	9		do. 1 O.R. on Leave.	J.E.W.
"	10th		do. 2 O.Rs proceeded on Leave to U.K. – 2 O.Rs. from Hospital – 3. O.Rs from Leave.	J.E.W.
"	11th		Work as above – 2 O.Rs on leave – Cpl. Brown proceeded to St. OMER to report to No 1 Aircraft Depot R.F.C. with a view to transferring to R.F.C.	J.E.W.
"	12th		3 Sections working on Forward Areas on Dug Outs new Battalion Headquarters 2 Sections " on Back areas on erection of Winter Quarters – 2 O.Rs from Leave 2. O.Rs on leave to U.K. 1 O.R. from Hospital	J.E.W.

1875 Wt. W593/826 1,000,000 4/15 J.B.C. & A. A.D.S.S./Forms/C. 2118.

Instructions regarding War Diaries and Intelligence Summaries are contained in F. S. Regs., Part II. and the Staff Manual respectively. Title Pages will be prepared in manuscript.

WAR DIARY
or
~~INTELLIGENCE~~ SUMMARY
(Erase heading not required.)

Army Form C. 2118

Place	Date	Hour	Summary of Events and Information	Remarks and references to Appendices
LEBUCQUIERE	13.9.17		Work as before. 3 Sections on work in Forward Area 1 Section on work in Back area. 2 O.R.s on leave to U.K. - 2 O.R.s rejoined from leave	J.E.D.
"	14.9.17		Work as above - 2 O.R. on leave to U.K.	J.E.D.
"	15.9.17		do do.	J.E.D.
"	16.9.17		Work as above. 1. O.R. to Hospital - 4 O.R.s proceeded on leave	J.E.D.
"	17.9.17		Work as above. 1 O.R. to Hospital - 1 O.R. from Hospital - 1 OR from leave	J.E.D.
			3. O.R.s on leave to U.K.	J.E.D.
"	18.9.17		Work as above. - 1 O.R. from Hospital. 2 O.R.s leave to U.K.	
"	19.9.17		Work as above. 6 O.R.s leave to U.K. - Corpl Brown A.B. returned from No 2 Aircraft Depot R.F.C. - 2. O.R.s rejoined from leave.	J.E.D.
"	20.9.17		Work as above. - 3. O.R.s leave to U.K.	J.E.D.
"	21.9.17		" " " 4. O.R.s leave to U.K. - 2. O.R.s returned from leave.	J.E.D.
"	22.9.17		Work as above. 5. O.R.s leave to U.K. -	J.E.D.
"	23.9.17		Work as above. 3 O.R.s leave to U.K. - 2 O.R.s from leave.	J.E.D.
"	24.9.17		Work as above. 3 O.Rs. leave - 1 O.R. from leave. Sappers Reeve and Petley relieved from work on LOUVERVAL WELL rejoined the Company. 3. O.R.s reinforcement from Base. - 1 O.R. to Hospital - The section working in Back areas put on to strengthening cellars in BEAUMETZ with a view to a possible bombardment of the village.	J.E.D.

1875 Wt. W593/826 1,000,000 4/15 J.B.C. & A. A.D.S.S./Forms/C. 2118.

Army Form C. 2118

Instructions regarding War Diaries and Intelligence Summaries are contained in F. S. Regs., Part II. and the Staff Manual respectively. Title Pages will be prepared in manuscript.

WAR DIARY
or
~~INTELLIGENCE SUMMARY~~

(Erase heading not required.)

Place	Date	Hour	Summary of Events and Information	Remarks and references to Appendices
LEBUCQUIERE	25.9.17.		2 Sections working in Forward Area on Dug Outs – 1 Section on new Battalion Headquarters and 1 Section on clearing + strengthening cellars BEAUMETZ.	JEW
"	26.9.17.		work as above. 4 O.Rs on Leave to U.K. – 1. OR Returned from Leave.	JEW
"	27.9.17		work as above. 1 O.R. to Hospital. 3. O.Rs on Leave to U.K. – 3 O.R.S returned from Leave.	JEW
"	28.9.17.		work as above. – 2 O.Rs on Leave to U.K. – 5. O.Rs. from Leave. 1. O.R. returned from Hospital	JEW
"	29.9.17		Work as above – 3 O.Rs on Leave to U.K. – 3 O.Rs from Leave.	JEW
"	30.9.17		Gas alarm sounded at 9.30 am. Enemy gas reported North of the CAMBRAI Road. work as above – 3. O.R.s on Leave to U.K.. 1 O.R. returned from Leave.	JEW

J. Ella Capt RE.
for MAJOR RE.
O.C. 513th (London) Field Co RE

1875 Wt. W593/826 1,000,000 4/15 J.B.C. & A. A.D.S.S./Forms/C. 2118.

Secret

Instructions regarding War Diaries and Intelligence Summaries are contained in F. S. Regs., Part II. and the Staff Manual respectively. Title Pages will be prepared in manuscript.

WAR DIARY
or
INTELLIGENCE SUMMARY
(Erase heading not required.)

Army Form C. 2118

513 Fd Coy R.E.

Vol 20

Place	Date	Hour	Summary of Events and Information	Remarks and references to Appendices
LEBUCQUIERE				
"	1.10.17		2 Sections working on Forward areas on Mine Dug Outs and Shelters – One Section on new Battalion HQ and 1 Section on cleaning & strengthening cellars, BEAUMETZ. – 1 O.R. to Hospital – 4 O.Rs on leave – 2 O.Rs from leave	J.E.O.
"	2.10.17		do. do. 1 O.R. on Sanitary Course PERONNE. – 1 O.R. to Hospital 3 O.Rs on leave to U.K. 8 O.Rs from leave.	J.E.O. J.E.O.
"	3.10.17		Work as above 1 O.R. from Hospital. 2 O.Rs on leave to U.K. – 1 O.R. from leave	J.E.O.
"	4.10.17		Work as above Sapper CAPP transferred to R.E. Signal Depot Advanced Base, ABBEVILLE – 3 O.Rs leave to U.K. – 6 O.Rs from leave – 41 O.Rs Infantry, attached to us as a Permanent Working Party. – 1 O.R.	J.E.O. J.E.O.
"	5.10.17		from Hospital – 2 O.Rs leave to U.K. – 2 O.R's from leave – 2 O.Rs from Base	J.E.O.
"	6.10.17		Work as above – ~~4~~ Nil O.Rs from leave – 2 O.R's Reinforcement from Base 3 O.Rs from leave.	J.E.O.
"	7.10.17		Company Rest day – Rifle & Box Respirator Inspection – 3 O.R. on leave to U.K. 3 O.Rs from leave	J.E.O.
"	8.10.17		No change in sectional work. Work as above. – Lt. MACFARLANE & 1 O.R. proceeded on leave to U.K. – CQMS Foster reported to this company with orders to be attached to us as per authority DAG's CR 5100/49/C. ~~Lt MACFARLANE proceeded on leave~~	J.E.O.

Army Form C. 2118

WAR DIARY
or
INTELLIGENCE SUMMARY
(Erase heading not required.)

Instructions regarding War Diaries and Intelligence Summaries are contained in F. S. Regs., Part II. and the Staff Manual respectively. Title Pages will be prepared in manuscript.

Place	Date	Hour	Summary of Events and Information	Remarks and references to Appendices
LEBUCQUIERE	9th		2 Sections working in forward area - one Section of new Bde H.Q. Shelters and one Section on Strengthening cellars. - 2 O.Rs rejoined from Leave	GEW
"	10th		work as above - 1. O.R. on Leave - 1. O.R. to Hospital.	GEW
"	11th		do do 1. O.R. on Leave - 2 O.Rs from Leave	GEW
"	12th		do do 5. O.Rs from Leave - 1 O.R. on Leave.	GEW
"	13th		do do 6. O.Rs. rejoined from Leave	GEW
"	14th		Company Rest day 3. O.Rs rejoined from Leave. - Gas Helmet, Box Respirator & Rifle Inspection	GEW
"	15th		do do 1. O.Rs rejoined from Leave - 1. O.R. granted 1 months Leave	GEW
"	16th		do do 3. O.Rs from Leave.	GEW
"	17th		do do 1. O.Rs. from Leave.	GEW
"	18th		do do 1. O.R. from Leave.	GEW
"	19th		do. do. 2. O.Rs. from Leave	GEW
"	20th		do do.	GEW
"	21st		do do. 1. O.R from Leave.	GEW
"	22nd		do do. 1. O.R to Hospital. 1 O.R. from Leave. MAJOR. G.T. KINGSFORD proceeded on Leave to U.K. Operations - Raid attempted on the German Trenches on the night 21/22nd. Sappers Hedgell & Thomas were detailed to take part in supplying & blowing up the enemy line by a Bangalore Torpedo. The raid failed owing to the enemy being on the alert. The Sappers returned to the company on the morning of the 22nd.	GEW
"	23rd		Company Rest day - Gas Helmet Box Respirator & Rifle Inspection 3. O.Rs from Leave	GEW

Instructions regarding War Diaries and Intelligence Summaries are contained in F. S. Regs., Part II. and the Staff Manual respectively. Title Pages will be prepared in manuscript.

WAR DIARY
or
INTELLIGENCE SUMMARY
(Erase heading not required.)

Army Form C. 2118

Place	Date	Hour	Summary of Events and Information	Remarks and references to Appendices
LEBUCQUIÈRE	24th.		One Section (No. 3) moved to forward area (LOUVERVAL) for work on new Company headquarters behind the front line. No. 2 Section work on Machine Gun Dugouts and Emplacements in Intermediate Line. No. 4 Section work on Intermediate Line. No. [illegible] Section work on Back areas for C.R.E.	[illegible]
"	25th.		Work as above – 1 O.R. from Leave – 1 O.R. to Hospital.	[illegible]
"	26th.		Work as above. 1 O.R. sent to attend a School of Cookery at ALBERT.	[illegible]
"	27th.		Work as above.	[illegible]
"	28th.		Work as above.	[illegible]
"	29th.		Work as above – 1 O.R. rejoined unit from Base Depot. – Lt. DAIN proceeded on 10 days leave to U.K.	[illegible]
"	30th.		Work as above.	[illegible]
"	31st.		Work as above. 2 O.Rs. proceeded on 14 days leave to U.K. (sailing on the 1st. Nov.).	[illegible]

[signature]
Captain, R.E.
O.C. 518 Field Co.
2. 11. 17.

1875 Wt. W593/826 1,000,000 4/15 J.B.C. & A. A.D.S.S./Forms/C. 2118.

Secret

Instructions regarding War Diaries and Intelligence Summaries are contained in F. S. Regs., Part II. and the Staff Manual respectively. Title pages will be prepared in manuscript.

WAR DIARY
or
~~INTELLIGENCE SUMMARY.~~
(Erase heading not required.)

Vol 21

Army Form C. 2118.

513 (London) Field Coy R.E.

Place	Date	Hour	Summary of Events and Information	Remarks and references to Appendices
			WORK.	
LEBUCQUIERE	1st Nov.		No 3 Section employed on Mine Dug outs in Front Line system of Trenches - Billets in cut & cover shelters in LOUVERVAL - No 2 Section on Machine Gun Emplacements and Dug outs No 4 Section work on Intermediate Line - No 1 Section on works for C.R.E. in Back areas	JEW
"	2nd	"	WORK as above	JEW
"	3rd	"	WORK as above. Major KINGSFORD RE. returned from Leave - 1 O.R. from Leave - 4 O.Rs proceeded on Leave to U.K.	JEW
"	4th	"	Redistribution of WORK. - No 3 Section employed on Mine Dug Outs in Front Line system of Trenches - Nos. 2 & 4 Section on Special R.E. Training - No 1 Section on works for C.R.E. in Back areas. - 1 O.R. from Leave.	JEW
"	5th	"	Work as above. - 3 O.Rs Leave to U.K - 1 O.R. to Hospital.	JEW
"	6th	"	Work as above - 3 O.Rs Leave to U.K - 1 O.R. from Hospital	JEW
"	7th	"	Work as above - 1 O.R. to Hospital.	JEW
"	8th	"	Work as above.	JEW
"	9th	"	Inter-section reliefs - No 2 Section employed on Mine Dug outs in Front Line System of Trenches - Nos 1 and 3 Sections employed on Special R.E. Training, No 4 Section on work for C.R.E. in Back areas. - 3 O.Rs leave to U.K.	JEW
"	10th		Work as above. - 1 O.R. to Hospital - 1 O.R. transferred to C.R.E.	JEW
"	11th		work as above - 1 O.R. to Hospital	JEW
"	12th		work as above - 1 O.R. from Hospital - 3 O.Rs leave to U.K.	JEW
"	13th		work as above.	JEW
"	~~13th~~			

D. D. & L., London, E.C. (A8004) Wt. W1771/M2 31 750,000 5/17 Sch. 52 Forms/C2118/14

Instructions regarding War Diaries and Intelligence Summaries are contained in F. S. Regs., Part II. and the Staff Manual respectively. Title pages will be prepared in manuscript.

WAR DIARY
or
~~INTELLIGENCE~~ SUMMARY.
(*Erase heading not required.*)

Army Form C. 2118.

Place	Date	Hour	Summary of Events and Information	Remarks and references to Appendices
LEBUCQUIERE	14th Nov.		Section 2 in Forward Areas – work on new Company Headquarters (Mined Dug Outs) Section 4 on Back area work – Sections 1 & 3 on Training in Trestle Bridging – 40 O.Rs attached to the Company for Operations in addition to the 40 already working for forward Section – 1 O.R rejoined from Hospital – 3 O.Rs leave to U.K	J.E.W. J.E.W.
"	15th Nov.		Work as above – 1 O.R. to Hospital	
"	16th Nov.		Redistribution of work – No 2 Section with 20 Attached Infantry on Mine Dug outs. Nos 1 & 3 Sections working on Corduroying BAPAUME–CAMBRAI Road LOUVERVAL Section – No 4 Section on construction and erection of Bridge No 10 to be erected in forthcoming Operations across the CANAL DU NORD – Site of Practice Erection – VELU CHATEAU Grounds – 20 more attached infantry joined the Company making the total 100 O.Rs – 1 O.R. Leave to U.K. – 1 O.R. to Bridging School AIRE	J.E.W.
"	17th Nov.		Work as above – erection of Bridge complete – inspection by G.O.C. 51st Divn & CRE.	J.E.W.
"	18th Nov.		Work as above – spare Bridge for same site as above taken and dumped at BOURSIES.	J.E.W.
"	19th Nov.		Work as above – Bridge No 10 erected in VELU CHATEAU grounds dismantled ready for removal – Today is Y day of operations.	J.E.W.
"	20th Nov.		Zero day of operations – Zero Hour 6.20 A.M. – No 1 Section on CAMBRAI Road, No 2 Sectn attached to Bde for operations – Nos 3 and 4 Sections standing by to erect bridge over canal – 3 O.Rs joined from Base 4 O.Rs from leave.	J.E.W. J.E.W.
"	21st Nov.		No 1 Sectn on Roads No 2 attached to Bde.	J.E.W.
"	22nd Nov.		do do . 1 O.R. from Leave – 1 O.R joined Coy. from Base	J.E.W.

D. D. & L., London, E.C. (A8094) Wt. W1771/M2 31 750,000 3/17 Sch. 52 Forms/C2118/14

Instructions regarding War Diaries and Intelligence Summaries are contained in F. S. Regs., Part II. and the Staff Manual respectively. Title pages will be prepared in manuscript.

Army Form C. 2118.

WAR DIARY
or
~~INTELLIGENCE SUMMARY.~~
(Erase heading not required.)

Place	Date	Hour	Summary of Events and Information	Remarks and references to Appendices
LEBUCQUIERE	23rd Nov.		No 1 section working on BAPAUME CAMBRAI Road – No 2 attached to Bde No 3 & 4 erecting Bridge across the CANAL DU NORD. 3 ORs rejoined from leave	JEW
"	24th Nov		Nos 1, 3 and 4 Sections on Road. No 2 attached to Bde. 2 ORs rejoined from leave. 1 OR proceeded on leave. – 1 OR killed. 1 OR wounded	JEW
"	25th Nov		do do 3 ORs rejoined from leave	JEW
"	26th Nov.		Work on roads handed over to 2nd Division 4 Sections attached to Bde – No 1, 3 & 4 sections working for Bde on wiring & digging new C.T. – 1 OR wounded. Nos 1, 3, and 4 Sections & attached Infantry moved up to Intermediate Line –	JEW
"	27th Nov		4 Sections working for Bde on wiring support line & supervising Infantry digging parties. Capt Vicks left on leave to UK.	JEW
"	28 Nov		Sections & infantry employed on own camping arrangements. 1 OR from Hospital	
"	29 Nov		Sections & infantry employed on construction of dugouts in Reserve line & deepening same. 1 OR to hospital 1 OR rejoined from Base.	G.T.K.
"	30 Nov		HQ & Transport lines moved from LEBUCQUIERE to transport lines of 189 Bde. Sections & Infantry employed as above. 1 OR wounded – 1 OR from leave – 1 OR proceeded on leave to UK. 1 OR to hospital.	G.T.K.

[signature]
MAJOR R.E.
O.C. 513 FIELD COY. R.E.

D. D. & L., London, E.C. (A8004) Wt. W1771/M2 31 750,000 5/17 Sch. 52 Forms/C2118/14

Secret

Instructions regarding War Diaries and Intelligence Summaries are contained in F. S. Regs., Part II. and the Staff Manual respectively. Title pages will be prepared in manuscript.

WAR DIARY
or
~~INTELLIGENCE SUMMARY.~~
(Erase heading not required.)

Army Form C. 2118.

513 Field Company RE

Vol 22

Place	Date	Hour	Summary of Events and Information	Remarks and references to Appendices
LEBUCQUIERE	Dec. 1st		Company employed wiring old enemy outpost line for defence as support line consequent upon enemy counterattack. 1 OR wounded - 2 OR rejoined from leave 1 OR to Hospital	GJK
	2nd		Company prepared to move. 1 OR rejoined from Bridging School 3 OR joined from Base 1 OR proceeded on leave	GJK
DAINVILLE	3rd		Company moved to Dainville. Transport under command of Lt Dain by road - dismounted personnel under O.C. by train to BEAUMETZ. 1 OR rejoined from leave 1 OR proceeded on leave	TDC
DAINVILLE	4th		Company at rest.	GJK
MAROEUIL	5		Company moved by road with 169 Bde to billets - MAROEUIL	TDC
"	6		Company at rest 1 OR proceeded on leave 1 OR rejoined from Hospital	GJK
ECURIE	7		Company moved to ECURIE & took over from 211 Fd Coy RE. 1 OR rejoined from Hospital 1 OR to hospital 1 OR proceeded on leave	GJK
	8th		No 1 3 & 4 Sections moved to dugouts near BAILLEUL under command of Lt Dain. Company employed wiring Red line 1 OR to hospital 1 OR leave	TDC
	9th		Company continued wiring 1 OR rejoined from Hospital Lt HARVEY proceeded on leave	TDC
	10th		" " " 1 OR proceeded on leave	TDC

D. D. & L., London, E.C. (A8004) Wt. W1771/M2-31 750,000 5/17 Sch: 52 Forms/C2118/14

Army Form C. 2118.

Instructions regarding War Diaries and Intelligence Summaries are contained in F. S. Regs., Part II. and the Staff Manual respectively. Title pages will be prepared in manuscript.

WAR DIARY
or
INTELLIGENCE SUMMARY.
(Erase heading not required.)

Place	Date	Hour	Summary of Events and Information	Remarks and references to Appendices
ECURIE	Dec 11		Company employed wiring Support line. 1 OR on leave 2 OR to hospital	T.J.K
	12		" " " " " 1 OR on leave 1 OR returned from leave 1 OR Hospital	T.J.K
	13		" " " " " 2 Lt Palmer 22 London Regt transferred to R.E. & posted to 513 Field Coy. Lt Pinnock attached to XIII Corps for wiring scheme	GJK
	14		Company employed wiring. 2/Lt Palmer to Veterinary Course Abbeville – Capt Villa rejoined from leave – 1 OR leave to UK 1 OR to Hospital	T.J.K
	15		Company completed wiring of front line Capt Villa proceeded to 231 Field Coy RE to command 1 OR to Hospital	GJK
	16		Company Rest day –	
	17		Company employed on provision of additional accommodation in RED LINE for wiring battalion & alterations & extensions at Divisional H.Q. 2 OR leave to UK	T.J.K
	18		Company employed as above 1 OR returned from leave 2 OR leave to UK	T.J.K
	19		" " " " Lt Pinnock proceeded on leave – 1 OR from leave 2 OR from Hospital	GJK
St CATHERINE ARRAS.	20		Company moved HQ to St Catherines & forward HQ to H 1 d 2 4 near ARRAS – BAILLEUL Road on part of Divisional front being handed over – Work on accommodation continued 1 OR from leave 2 OR on leave to UK	GJK
	21		Company worked on forward accommodation & Divisional H.Q. 1 OR on leave 1 OR from Hospital	GJK

D. D. & L., London, E.C. (A8004) Wt. W1771/M2 31 750,000 5/17 Sch. 52 Forms/C2118/14

Instructions regarding War Diaries and Intelligence Summaries are contained in F. S. Regs., Part II. and the Staff Manual respectively. Title pages will be prepared in manuscript.

WAR DIARY
or
INTELLIGENCE SUMMARY.
(Erase heading not required.)

Army Form C. 2118.

Place	Date	Hour	Summary of Events and Information	Remarks and references to Appendices
	Dec.			
St Catherine	22		Work continued on accommodation phrases & task. 2OR leave to UK	G.T.K
	23		Work as above continued 1 OR proceeded on leave to UK	G.T.K
	24		Work as above. 1OR from leave 1 OR to leave	G.T.K
	25		Company rest Day 1 OR on leave to UK	G.T.K
	26		Work begun in making & revetting firebays in MARINE . NAVAL TRENCHES & RED LINE 1 OR returned from Hospital 1 OR to leave. 2 OR to Hospital	G.T.K
	27.		Work continued as above 1 OR to leave	G.T.K
	28		" " " " 1 OR returned from leave 1 OR to UK on leave	G.T.K
	29		" " " " Lt Palmer & 1OR returned from Veterinary Course Lt ASH proceeded to 1st Army School – 1OR from Hospital 1 OR to UK on leave	G.T.K
	30		Work continued on MARINE . NAVAL Trenches & RED LINE. New dugout for MG. off MARINE TRENCH started – 1 OR from leave 1 OR to leave	G.T.K
	31		Work as above. 1 OR returned from leave	G.T.K

G.T. Kingsford
Maj. RE
OC 573 Fd Coy RE

D. D. & L., London, E.C. (A8004) Wt. W1771/M2 31 750,000 5/17 Sch. 52 Forms/C2118/14

Instructions regarding War Diaries and Intelligence Summaries are contained in F. S. Regs., Part II. and the Staff Manual respectively. Title Pages will be prepared in manuscript.

SECRET

WAR DIARY
or
~~INTELLIGENCE SUMMARY~~
(Erase heading not required.)

Army Form C. 2118

513 Field Company RE

Vol 23

Place	Date	Hour	Summary of Events and Information	Remarks and references to Appendices
St CATHARINES ARRAS	1918 Jan 1		Coy rest day. Baths – Box Respirator drill Rifle inspection etc. 2 O.R. from leave 1 O.R. on leave. 3 O.R. joined from Base Depot	CHRB
	2		Three Sections attached to 169 Infantry Brigade employed on Dug-out work in THAMES and TOWY CTs No 4 Section on Roads and back area work 1 O.R. on leave to U.K. 2 O.R. from leave. 1 O.R. went to Hospital.	CHRB
	3		Work as above. 2nd Lt Palmer takes over work on XIII Corps Roads 2nd Lt McGILL proceeds on leave to U.K. Lt PINNOCK returns from leave.	CHRB
	4		Work as above. 1 O.R. from leave. 1 O.R. from Base Depot	CHRB
	5		Work as above 1 O.R from leave	CHRB
	6		Coy relieved by 461st Coy and moves to AUBREY CAMP Horse line in St CATHARINES. 2 O.R. on leave. 1 O.R. to XIII Corps Gas Course	CHRB
	7		Coy employed on wiring scheme for XIII Corps. 1 and 3 Sections wiring NORTH of CHANTECLER SWITCH – 2 and 4 Sections working SOUTH of the SWITCH. 1 O.R. on leave – 1 O.R. from leave.	CHRB
	8		Work as above all 4 Sections working South of SWITCH. 2 O.R. from leave 2 O.R. on leave	CHRB

Instructions regarding War Diaries and Intelligence Summaries are contained in F. S. Regs., Part II. and the Staff Manual respectively. Title Pages will be prepared in manuscript.

WAR DIARY
or
~~INTELLIGENCE SUMMARY~~
(Erase heading not required.)

Army Form C. 2118

513 Field Coy

Place	Date	Hour	Summary of Events and Information	Remarks and references to Appendices
ST. CATHARINE ARRAS	1918 Jan 9		Work for XIII Corps cont: 1 and 3 Section working NORTH of SWITCH 2 and 4 working SOUTH of SWITCH. 2. OR on leave. 1 OR. from leave	CHPS
	10		Work as above. PTE KELLETT RAMC attached on leave	CHPS
	11		Work as above. 2nd LT HARVEY wounded and goes to No 30 C.C.S. 2 O.R. on leave. 1 OR from leave. 1. O.R. from Hospital.	CHPS
	12		Coy rest day Baths Box Respirator drill. 3. OR. on leave. 2nd LT PALMER on leave	CHPS
	13		work for XIII Corps cont: 2. O.R. on leave {1 O.R. from leave / 1 OR. from gas course. 1 O.R to HOSPITAL	CHPS
	14		work as above 1 O.R. from leave. 3 O.R on leave 2 O.R. to Hospital	CHPS
	15		work as above. 1 O.R on leave. 1 OR. to Hospital	CHPS
	16		Work as above 2. OR on leave	CHPS
	17		work as above. 2 OR. to Hospital	CHPS
	18		work as above LT. BOURNE rejoined from Base Depot and resumes command of No 2 Section 2nd LT KIDMAN joined from Base Depot.	CHPS
	19		work as above for XIII Corps. II LT McGILL returns from leave. 1 OR from leave	CHPS
	20		Work as above cont.	CHPS
	21		Work as above cont: Sergt Rutherford JJ proceeds to UK to report to WAR Office	CHPS

Army Form C. 2118.

Instructions regarding War Diaries and Intelligence Summaries are contained in F. S. Regs., Part II. and the Staff Manual respectively. Title Pages will be prepared in manuscript.

WAR DIARY
or
INTELLIGENCE SUMMARY

(Erase heading not required.)

Place	Date	Hour	Summary of Events and Information	Remarks and references to Appendices
St. CATHARINES · ARRAS ·	1918 · JAN ·			
	22 ·		Work for XIII Corps continued – ~~Sergt Rutherford proceeds to U.K. to R.E. Cadet Batt.~~ 1·OR· leave to U.K. – 1·OR· rejoined from Hospital – 1·OR· rejoined from leave.	W.A.R.B.
	23 ·		Work as above. – Major Kingsford becomes actg C.R.E. – 1·OR· rejoined from leave. – 1·OR· rejoined from Hospital. 1·OR· leave to U.K.	W.A.R.B.
	24 ·		Infty. Relief – Coy. Rest Day – Baths – Inspection of Rifles & Box Respirators. 1·OR· leave to U.K. 2·OR· rejoin from Hospital – 4·OR· rejoin from leave. – B.G.G.S. XIII Corps visits Corps Wiring Scheme & sites new M.G. Positions.	W.A.R.B.
	25		Coy. employed on removing old wire & wiring on M.G. Rays as sited by Corps B.G.G.S. 1·OR· leave to UK. – II Lieut A.V. Kidman takes command of No. 3. Section during Lieut Macfarlane's Tour of duty on Horse Lines.	W.A.R.B.
	26 ·		Work as above – B.G.G.S XIII Corps visited works · 1·OR· leave to UK. – 4·OR· Reinforcements from Base Depot.	W.A.R.B.
	27 ·		Work as above – 5·OR· rejoin from leave – 1·OR· leave to UK.	W.A.R.B.
	28 ·		Work as above – II Lieut K. Palmer rejoins from leave. – 1·OR· rejoins from leave.	W.A.R.B.
	29 ·		Work as above. – Major J.J. Kingsford rejoins the Unit – 2·OR· leave to U.K. –	W.A.R.B.

2449 Wt. W14957/M90 750,000 1/16 J.B.C. & A. Forms/C.2118/12.

WAR DIARY
or
~~INTELLIGENCE SUMMARY.~~
(Erase heading not required.)

Army Form C. 2118.

Instructions regarding War Diaries and Intelligence Summaries are contained in F. S. Regs., Part II. and the Staff Manual respectively. Title pages will be prepared in manuscript.

Place	Date	Hour	Summary of Events and Information	Remarks and references to Appendices
ST CATHARINES ARRAS	1918 JAN			
	30		Work for XIII Corps continued. 1 OR rejoins from leave.	W.A.R.B.
	31		Work till 1-30% p.m as above. - Company attends lecture by C.R.E. in afternoon. - 1 OR rejoins from Hospital. - 1 OR transferred to 25th A.T. Coy. R.E.	W.A.R.B.

G.T.T. [illegible]
Major RE
OC 573 Field Coy RE.

(A7092). Wt. W12839/M1293. 75,0.0. 1/17. D. D. & L., Ltd. Forms/C.2118/14.

Secret

Instructions regarding War Diaries and Intelligence Summaries are contained in F. S. Regs., Part II. and the Staff Manual respectively. Title pages will be prepared in manuscript.

WAR DIARY or INTELLIGENCE SUMMARY. 513 FIELD COMPANY

(Erase heading not required.)

Army Form C. 2118.

Vol 24

Place	Date FEB	Hour	Summary of Events and Information	Remarks and references to Appendices
AUBREY CAMP ST CATHARINE	1.		Company rest day. Box Respirator drill. Baths etc. A clean change of clothing was obtained for the Company. 1 O.R. from leave. 2 O.R's on leave to U.K.	CHRL
	2		Working on XIIIth Corps defence Scheme. No's 1 and 2 Sections digging M.G. emplacements. No's 3 and 4 Sections cutting gaps in wire and making Knife Rests. 2 O.R's from leave	CHRL
	3		Work as above. No 1 Section completing wire round GAUL POST. No 2 Section on M.G. emplacements. No 3 and 4 Sections on cutting gaps. II LIEUT. ASH rejoins from 1st Army School. 2 O.R's on leave to U.K. 1 O.R from leave 2 O.R's to Hospital.	CHRL
	4		Work as above. 1 O.R from leave. 2 O.R's on leave. LIEUT. MACFARLANE on leave to U.K.	CHRL
	5		Work as above. B.G.G.S. inspected work and laid out some new work. 1 O.R on leave 1 O.R from leave. 2 O.R's attached 148 A.T. Coy R.E.	CHRL
	6		Work as above. No 1 Section on altering wire at H.8.b.50.95. No 2 Section on M.G. empts. No 3 Section on new wire round BLANCHE POST. No 4 Section on TONGUE POST. 1 O.R. from leave. 1 O.R. rejoins from Base.	CHRL
	7.		Work as above. Coy employed on Spit-locking Posts and Salving wire and tools. 1 O.R. from leave.	CHRL
	8.		Work as above. 2 Sections employed putting up Notice boards in gaps and completing Spit-locking of Posts. 1 O.R. Joined from Base.	CHRL

(A7092). Wt. W12839/M1293. 750,000. 1/17. D. D. & L., Ltd. Forms/C.2118/14.

Secret

Instructions regarding War Diaries and Intelligence Summaries are contained in F. S. Regs., Part II. and the Staff Manual respectively. Title pages will be prepared in manuscript.

WAR DIARY
or
~~INTELLIGENCE SUMMARY.~~

(Erase heading not required.)

Army Form C. 2118.

Place	Date	Hour	Summary of Events and Information	Remarks and references to Appendices
CHANTECLER Hid 1.7	FEBRUARY 9.		Coy relieve 461st Field Coy in the line. Four Sections and H.Q. move to forward billets at Hid 1.7. Mounted Section takes over HARDY Camp. II Lt McGILL in charge. II Lt. K PALMER to 1st Army Inf. School. 2 O.R. to Inf School. 1 O.R. on leave	CHRL
	10		Parade 8.30am Rifle inspection. Box Respirator drill. No 3 Section completed placing of notice boards in gaps in wire (XIII Corps defence scheme) officers and NCOs going round line. Cpl Green to Base. Repairs done to G.O.C. 169th Bde dug-out. Bath at CHANTECLER inspected	CHRL
	11		Company employed on Dugs Outs. Shift work. No 1 Section on dug out at B30a 9.8. for M.G. Coy. No II Section B29d 5.8. No III Section B29d 8.2 No IV B29b 8.1 Balance of men B29c 3.3.	CHRL
	12		Work continued as above 1 OR on leave. 1 OR from leave. 2 OR. from Base. 4 OR. Hospital	CHRL
	13.		Work as above Camp inspected by C.R.E. 3 O.R. from leave 1 OR Hospital. 1 OR. to C.R.E.	CHRL
	14		Work as above. C.R.E went round dug. Outs 2 OR. to Hospital 2 OR. from leave. 1 O.R. from Bridging School	CHRL
	15		Work as above. CRE inspected Horselines. Lt Bourne went round artillery work with Lt CARSON. R.A.R.E.	CHRL
	16		Lt BOURNE moves to G6d8.x with No 2 Section less 17 OR. attached to R.A. and rationed by them. 20. OR D.A.C attached to No 2 Section.	CHRL
	17.		Work as above. 1 officer and 75 O.R. attached to Coy from Q.W.R. 1 officer 75 O.R attached from 1/2nd LONDONS as permanent working party. 1 OR. from Hospital 2 OR. from Base. 1 OR on leave	CHRL
	18		Work as above. 1 OR from leave. 2 OR. from Base.	CHRL
	19.		Coy rest day. Clean change of clothing obtained. Rifle inspection. Gas drill and Kit inspection 2 O.R. from leave.	CHRL
	20		Work as above. 20 R. att RAMC. for dug. out work. 1 OR. from Hospital 2 OR on leave. Lt MACFARLANE rejoins from leave. O.C. goes to ~~[illegible]~~ Team lecture on economy at HOUDIN	CHRL

Secret

Instructions regarding War Diaries and Intelligence Summaries are contained in F. S. Regs., Part II. and the Staff Manual respectively. Title pages will be prepared in manuscript.

WAR DIARY
or
INTELLIGENCE SUMMARY.
(Erase heading not required.)

Army Form C. 2118.

Place	Date	Hour	Summary of Events and Information	Remarks and references to Appendices
	FEBRUARY			
CHANTECLER H.1d.1.7.	21		Work on dug-outs continued: 2 O.R. on leave to U.K. 1 O.R. rejoined from C.R.E. PTE KELLETT transferred to 2/3rd (LONDON) Field Ambulance in accordance with G.R.O. 3282. 1 O.R. to Hospital.	CHRL
	22		Work as above	CHRL
	23		Work as above 1.O.R to Hospital	CHRL
	24		Work as above 1 O.R. to Hospital	CHRL
	25		Work on dug-outs continued	CHRL
	26		Work on dug-outs continued. PELICAN. KEILLAR and CASTLEFORD posts dug to depth of 3'0". 1 O.R. joined from BASE DEPOT. 1 O.R to Hospital 1 O.R on leave	CHRL
	27		Work on dug-outs continued: 1 O.R. to Hospital. 1 O.R. on leave. 1 O.R from leave	CHRL
	28.		Coy rest day. Rifle inspection. Gas helmet drill. Baths and clean change of clothing. Party out improving Posts. Major KINGSFORD proceeds on 1 months leave to UK. 1 O.R on leave to U.K.	CHRL

CHR Lallin
Captain, R.E.
O/C. 513 Field Co.

(A7092) Wt W12839/M1293 75,000 1/17. D. D. & L., Ltd. Forms/C.2118/14.

56th Div.

WAR DIARY

513th FIELD COMPANY, R.E.

M A R C H

1 9 1 8

Secret

Instructions regarding War Diaries and Intelligence Summaries are contained in F. S. Regs., Part II. and the Staff Manual respectively. Title pages will be prepared in manuscript.

WAR DIARY
or
~~INTELLIGENCE SUMMARY.~~
(Erase heading not required.)

513 FIELD COMPANY

Vol 25

Army Form C. 2118.

Place	Date	Hour	Summary of Events and Information	Remarks and references to Appendices
	MARCH			
ARRAS	1.		Work on dug-outs continued. Dug-Out 127 Completed	CHRB
H1d17.	2		Work as above. The remainder of No 2 Section attached to R.A. and work with Lt BOURNE.	CHRB
	3		Work as above. Dug-outs continued. 1 O.R. to Hospital	CHRB
	4		Work on dug-outs continued. Party of Sappers covering THAMES BATTERY POST. 1 O.R. to Hospital. 3 O.R. to 1/5 Cheshire Regt for Course in LEWIS GUN	CHRB
	5.		Work on dug-Outs continued	CHRB
	6.		Work on dug-outs continued. 1 O.R. to hospital. 1 O.R. from leave. C.R.E. visited Camp.	CHRB
	7.		Work on dug-outs continued. 1 O.R. on leave. ~~No~~ Dug-outs 128 and 129 completed.	CHRB CHRB
	~~8~~		~~Work on dug-outs 130 and 33 continued. Taking over dug-out work from 176 Tunnelling Company~~	
	8.		Rest day. Baths and Clean change of clothing. Rifle and Box Respirator drill	~~CHRB~~
	9		New dug-outs commenced in RED LINE. Taken over from 176 Tunnelling Company. 65 O.R. attached from 167 Brigade. 80 O.R. return to their battalions (169 Bde) 2 O.R. on Course at LEWIS GUN instruction at FLORINGHAM. XIII Corps.	CHRB CHRB
	10.		Work on dug-Outs continued. 4 six hour shifts. 1 O.R. from leave. 1 O.R. transferred to No 7 Foreways Base depot SAVY. 1 O.R. to Hospital	CHRB
	11.		Work on dug-outs continued. Capt G. B. LaGAURDIA and 1 O.R. 2nd Corps School Engineer Section U.S.A. attached for instructional purposes 11/3/18. ~~Company~~ 1 O.R. to hospital. 6 O.R. gassed while working in dug-outs in TOWY and Red Line and go to hospital.	CHRB
	12		Work on dug-outs continued. Bridge prepared for demolition at H1d3.0. Company standing to from 5.0 am until daylight. 2 O.R. to hospital with shell gas. 2 O.R. from Hospital. Dug-Out handed over to 512 Field Coy	

(A7092). Wt W12839/M1293. 750,000. 1/17. D. D. & L., Ltd. Forms/C.2118/14.

Instructions regarding War Diaries and Intelligence Summaries are contained in F. S. Regs., Part II. and the Staff Manual respectively. Title pages will be prepared in manuscript.

WAR DIARY
or
INTELLIGENCE SUMMARY. 513 Field Company

(Erase heading not required.)

Army Form C. 2118.

Place	Date	Hour	Summary of Events and Information	Remarks and references to Appendices
ARRAS CHANTECLER H1.d1.7.	MARCH 13		Work on dug-outs continued: Company stand to at 5.0.a.m. until daylight 2 OR to hospital 1 OR from hospital	CHRB
	14		Work on dug outs continued: 1 OR to hospital. Company stand to at 5.0.a.m.	
	15		Work on dug outs continued. 1 OR to hospital 1 OR wounded (shrapnel)	CHRB
	16		Work on dug-out continued. 2 OR from hospital. 2 OR to hospital	CHRB
	17.		Work on dug-outs continued. Gas shells during night 16th-17th adjoining Billets. 1 O.R. from Hospital. 1 O.R. to Hospital. 1 O.R. from Leave. Corpl. Green returned to Base Depot. 1 O.R. Gas shell (wounded)	CHRB
	18.		Lieut. Palmer & 2 O.R. rejoins from 1st Army Infy Course. - work on dug-outs continued. 5 O.R. gas shell (wounded)	
	19.		Work on dug out continued. - No. 151. D out handed over to 512th Field Coy.	
	20.		do do do Lieut Kidman in conjunction with Ordnance Officer destroys old shells. 1 O.R. to Hospital.	
	21.		"Stand To" 5/0 a.m. work on dug-out continued. 1 O.R. wounded (Gas)	
	22.		Officers of 2nd Canadian Division come to "take over" II Lieut Kidman goes hospital (Gas). "Stand To" 5/0 a.m.	
	23		work on dug outs continued. 1 O.R. to Hospital. 1 O.R. wounded (Gas) "Stand To" 5/0 am II Lieut Ash to Hospital - work on dug-out ceases - 3 Sections wiring in front of NAVAL & MARINE Trenches 2 O.R. from Hospital 2 O.R. from Corps Musketry School.	
	24		"Stand To" 5/0 a.m. 3 Sections wiring NAVAL & MARINE Trenches.	
	25		"Stand To" 5/0 a.m. 3 Sections wiring NAVAL & MARINE Trenches. - handed over dug outs to officers of 176th Tunnelling Coy.	

(A7092). Wt. W12839/M1293 75,0.0. 1/17. D. D. & L., Ltd. Forms/C.2118/14.

Instructions regarding War Diaries and Intelligence Summaries are contained in F. S. Regs., Part II. and the Staff Manual respectively. Title pages will be prepared in manuscript.

WAR DIARY
or
~~INTELLIGENCE SUMMARY.~~
(Erase heading not required.)

513th Field Coy. RE.

Place	Date	Hour	Summary of Events and Information	Remarks and references to Appendices
ARRAS. CHANTECLER. H.1.d.1.7.	March 26		"Stand To" 4⁰/c a.m. 3 Sections deepening & joining up "Green Line" - Billets shelled in evening. 3 ORs wounded. 1 OR. from leave. Lieut Pinnock 1 OR. returns from XIII Corps.	[initials]
	27		Lieut Bourne rejoins - R.A.R.E. work ceases - work on "Green Line" continues - "Stand To" 4⁰/c a.m. Officers make reconnaissance of Redoubts in Rear Lines. 9 Sappers with three "Bangalore" Torpedoes take part in Raids 26th-27th.	[initials]
	28		"Stand To" 4⁰/c a.m. - heavy bombardment commences 3⁰/c am. - Reserve R.E. Brigade formed - Tool carts removed from forward billets at 8⁰/c am. to Horse lines - 4 Sections move to ~~[illegible]~~ JUNCTION REDOUBT through day & garrison TONGUE POST at 7⁰/c p.m. Lieut Macfarlane & 5 ORs. left at forward billets. 1 Section - cutting trench across GAVRELLE ROAD connecting RED LINE.	[initials]
	~~[illegible]~~ 29		Capt Dain M.C. R.E. takes over command of 416th Field Coy. Coy. withdrawn from TONGUE POST at 11⁰/c p.m. move to HARDY CAMP. 1 OR. to Hospital.	[initials]
	30		Bridge Demolition Scheme handed over with area maps & other Coy work in hand to Officer of 12th Canadian Field Coy. Lieut Macfarlane & 7 OR. return HARDY CAMP. - 4 Section move	WARB
			at 11⁰/c am. to Billets at ANZIN. 2 OR. from R.E. Park MAROEUIL. 1 OR. to Hospital.	WARB
ANZIN. G.7b.5.9.	31.		Kit Inspection & Baths.	

W.A.R. Bourne.
Lieut R.E.
O/C 513th Field Coy. R.E.

(A7092). Wt W12839/M1293. 75,0 0. 1/17. D. D. & L., Ltd. Forms/C.2118/14.

56th Divisional Engineers

513rd FIELD COMPANY R. E.

APRIL 1918.

SECRET

513th FIELD COY R.E.

Army Form C. 2118.

WAR DIARY
or
INTELLIGENCE SUMMARY.

(Erase heading not required.)

Instructions regarding War Diaries and Intelligence Summaries are contained in F. S. Regs., Part II. and the Staff Manual respectively. Title pages will be prepared in manuscript.

Vol 26

Place	Date APRIL	Hour	Summary of Events and Information	Remarks and references to Appendices
ANZIN-ST-AUBIN G.7.b.4.9.	1st		Infantry Training in morning under Section Officers – 10 O.R. (Cheshire Pioneers) return to Batt: 1 O.R. to Hospital. 1 O.R. returns from Hospital.	W.A.R.B.
	2nd		Infantry Training in morning – shelling at intervals through night 1st/2nd & also through day. 2nd Lieut E. J. GILES R.E. reports for duty from R.E. Base Depot. – 1 O.R. returns from Hospital. 1 Officer + 1 O.R. attached from 1st London Regt. for instructional purposes in Infantry Training.	W.A.R.B.
	3rd		Infantry Training in morning. 1 O.R. to Hospital – 7 O.R. Attached Infty. rejoin Batt (L.R.B.) – 2nd Lieut CHAMBERS R.F. + 34 O.R. rejoin Batt. (2nd London Regt.) – 11 O.R. Reinforcements arrive from R.E. Base Depot.	W.A.R.B.
	4th		Infantry Training continued – C.R.E. visits Coy. H.Q. – 1 O.R. rejoins from Hospital.	W.A.R.B.
	5th		Coy. moves to ESTREE-CAUCHIE arriving 2 o/c p.m. – C.R.E. visits billets.	W.A.R.B.
ESTREE-CAUCHIE W.2.a.	6th		Physical Drill in morning – packing of vehicles in afternoon in view of move.	W.A.R.B.
	7th		Move to AGNEZ-LES-DUISSANS – 3rd Canadian Field Coy. left billets on arrival of this Coy. so impossible to take over. – Capt Bourne R.E. visits office of C.E. XVII Corps + goes over DAINVILLE Defence Line with Major Horton R.E.	W.A.R.B.
AGNEZ-LES-DUISSANS K.12.b.2.7.	8th		Coy. starts work on DAINVILLE DEFENCE LINE – Coy acting on instructions from XVII Corps. moves to WAGNONLIEU.	W.A.R.B.
WAGNONLIEU. L.22.c.1.8.	9th		Coy. continues work on DAINVILLE LINE – Coy under Capt. Bourne (with Lieut Pinnock 2nd Lieuts. Palmer & Giles) less Nos. 3 + 4 Sections move to RONVILLE CAVES – No. 3 Section & Mounted Section under Lieut Macfarlane (with 2nd Lieut Megill) remain at WAGNONLIEU. – No. 4 Section under 2nd Lieut Kidman move to WARLUS. K.36.d. for work on D.H.Q. – 1 O.R. rejoins Coy. from C.R.E.s Office.	W.A.R.B.
RONVILLE CAVES G.34.b.56.48.	10th		Work on DAINVILLE LINE continues – No. 4 Section start work on mined Dug-out for Div. H.Q. Signals – Nos. 1 + 2 Sections start work on Gas Doors, Latrines etc in connection with RONVILLE CAVE System. Lieut Giles starts reconnaissance of Cave System (exits entrances). Sanitary Officer i/c Cave System calls sappers to site position of Latrines throughout. Stand to 5 o/c A.M. 1 O.R. to Hospital. 1 O.R. to C.R.E.s Office. Lieut Smallman & servant return to 1st London Regt.	W.A.R.B.
	11th		All work as above (April 10th) continued – Reconnaissance of Dug-outs in Div: Area taken over from E. 416th F. Coy. – C.R.E. visits Coy. H.Q. – Stand to 5 o/c a.m. also 10-30 o/c to 11-15 o/c A.M. – Gas encountered at intervals through early morning & night (Respirators worn) – 1 O.R. to Hospital (gas).	W.A.R.B.
	12th		All work as above continued with (April 11th) – Lieut Pinnock takes over ACHICOURT BRIDGE Demolition Scheme (G.33.c.4.0.) from Canadian O.R.C. Coy. + places 1 Sapper on site to take charge – he also places 1 Sapper on site of CRINCHON BRIDGE (G.32.b.9.1.) demolition charges not yet completed by 25th Tunnelling Coy. R.E. – C.R.E. visits Horse Lines. 1 O.R. to hospital.	W.A.R.B.

(A7092). Wt W12539/M1293 75,000 1/17. D. D. & L., Ltd. Forms/C.2118/14.

SECRET.

513th FIELD COY. R.E.

Instructions regarding War Diaries and Intelligence Summaries are contained in F. S. Regs., Part II. and the Staff Manual respectively. Title pages will be prepared in manuscript.

WAR DIARY
or
~~INTELLIGENCE SUMMARY.~~
(Erase heading not required.)

Army Form C. 2118.

Place	Date APRIL	Hour	Summary of Events and Information	Remarks and references to Appendices
RONVILLE CAVES G-34.6.56.44	13th		All work as for 12th inst. continued with - Infantry Guards mounted on ACHICOURT & CRINCHON Bridges. O.C. Sanitation of Cave System sites latrine Positions with Lieut Pinnock. 1.OR. rejoins from hospital. 1.OR. reinforcement from R.E. Base Depot.	W.A.R.B.
	14th		Work as yesterday - II LIEUT McGILL attached to DIV. ARTILLERY - LIEUT. MACFARLANE takes over Horse Lines. Cave latrines started.	W.A.R.B.
	15th		Work as yesterday - Capt. Bourne + Lieut Pinnock meet O.C. + officers of 257 Tunnelling Coy at CRINCHON BRIDGE + discuss scheme of demolition. C.E. XVII Corps views Bridge + gives permission for removal of demolition charges placed by Railway Coy. 9.OR. report from R.E. Base Depot.	W.A.R.B.
	16th		Work as yesterday continued. 1.OR. to Hospital.	W.A.R.B.
	17th		Capt Bourne, Lieut Pinnock + II Lieut Giles with orderlies reconnoitre Battle Positions in ARRAS EAST DEFENCE LINE as instructed - later Lieut Macfarlane + mounted N.C.O.s shown Battle Positions by Capt Bourne. II Lieut Palmer visits Battle Positions + with II Lieut Giles reconnoitre overland + Sewer routes to RONVILLE CAVES. - work continued as yesterday. Battle Instructions issued to all detached officers + ~~[illegible]~~ arrangements discussed with all officers with H.Q. + Lieuts Macfarlane + Giles.	W.A.R.B.
	18th		Work as yesterday continued. Remainder of Officers + N.C.O.s visit Battle Positions - Major Rainy + Capt Bourne visit Battle Positions - Lieut Pinnock makes liaison with Lieut Bryce R.E. regarding evacuation of heavy guns over bridge. C.1. - work continued. 1.OR. to hospital.	W.A.R.B.
	19th		Work continued - Capt Bourne attends C.R.E. Conference - Lieuts Pinnock + Giles visit C.R.A. Brigade Major regarding evacuation of guns over ACHICOURT BRIDGE. - Major G. I. Kingsford rejoins from Sick Leave. 1.OR. to hospital.	W.A.R.B.
	20th		C.R.E. meets Lieuts Pinnock + Giles on sites of ACHICOURT + CRINCHON Bridges + discusses schemes of Demolition - thickness of abutments of ACHICOURT Bridge to be ascertained - this work commenced - other work continued. Sapper Beckett "wounded at Duty" - a good deal of intermittent enemy shelling throughout day.	W.A.R.B.
	21st		Work continued - No 3 Section rejoin Coy. from XVII. Corps, at RONVILLE CAVES - 1.OR. To Hospital.	W.A.R.B.
	22nd		Work continued - No 1 Section takes over work at WARLUS from No 4. Section who rejoin Coy H.Q. - 1.OR. to Hospital. - No 2 Section + Batt. evacuating wiring TILLOY RESERVE. Lieut Kidman R.E. takes over ACHICOURT BRIDGE Demolition.	W.A.R.B.
	~~22nd~~ 23rd		Work continued - forward area work taken over from 416th Field Coy. - No 3 Section continue work in Caves - No 4 Section with [illegible] wiring + dig NORTH ALLEY - No 2 Section resting - Lieut Kidman takes over from Lieut Brown (416th F. Coy) - New Battle Instructions received from CRE.	W.A.R.B.
	24th		Work in Caves continued - No. 2 Section work on Caves through night - No. 4 Section wiring + digging FICHEAUX SWITCH. 11 OR. Reinforcements arrive from R.E. Base Depot. No 1 Section shelled at WARLUS.	W.A.R.B.

(A7092) Wt. W12839/M1293 750,000 1/17 D. D. & L., Ltd. Forms/C.2118/14.

·SECRET·

513th FIELD·COY·R·E·

WAR DIARY
or
~~INTELLIGENCE~~ SUMMARY.
(Erase heading not required.)

Army Form C. 2118.

Instructions regarding War Diaries and Intelligence Summaries are contained in F. S. Regs., Part II. and the Staff Manual respectively. Title pages will be prepared in manuscript.

Place	Date APRIL	Hour	Summary of Events and Information	Remarks and references to Appendices
RONVILLE·CAVES G·34·b·56·48·	25th		Work on Screens - ~~Dugouts for Batts in line commenced~~ - No. 2 Section (Lieut Palmer) with 100 Infty wiring TILLOY RESERVE by night - No. 4 Section (2nd Lieut Kidman) with Batt: wiring & clearing out FICHEAUX·SWITCH - 4 OR wounded - 3 OR wounded at duty - 1 OR to hospital - 1 OR killed. Major & Captain visit Battle Positions	W.A.R.B.
	26th		Work continued as yesterday - Dugouts for Battalions in line commenced - Major attends Conference of B.G.C. 168th Bde.	W.A.R.B.
	27th		Work as yesterday - Nos. 2 & 4 Sections wiring - Latrine work in Cave System handed over to 512 Field Coy - 1 OR to hospital	W.A.R.B.
	28th		Nos. 2-3-4 Sections move with Coy. H.Q. to ARRAS. - Brigade Relief.	W.A.R.B.
ARRAS. G·27·b·15·90·			All technical work in RONVILLE CAVES handed over to 512th Field Coy - Wiring & Dug-out work continued - Capt Bowne R.E on Reconnaissance of ARRAS underground communications - C.R.E visits Coy H.Q. - 2 OR. to hospital.	W.A.R.B.
	29th		Nos. 2 & 4 Sections wiring FICHEAUX - RESERVE Line. - Infantry digging FICHEAUX-SWITCH - preparation of ACHICOURT Bridge demolition charges.	
			Work as yesterday - Reconnaissance of FICHEAUX-SWITCH made by Lieut Pinnock & 2nd Lieut Palmer - 1 OR to hospital - 1 OR wounded - Sentry on CRINCHON BRIDGE attacked by unknown enemy night April 30th - May 1st	W.A.R.B.

G. T. [illegible]
Major RE

Instructions regarding War Diaries and Intelligence Summaries are contained in F. S. Regs., Part II. and the Staff Manual respectively. Title pages will be prepared in manuscript.

513TH (LONDON) FIELD COY., R.E.
No ....
Date ....

WAR DIARY
or
~~INTELLIGENCE SUMMARY.~~
(Erase heading not required.)

Army Form C. 2118.

Vol 27

Place	Date MAY	Hour	Summary of Events and Information	Remarks and references to Appendices
ARRAS. G.27.b.15.90.	1st.		Nos: 2 + 4 Sections wiring by night - No: 3 Section on mined Dug-out repairs in TILLOY-LINE. - No 1 Section at WARLUS on Div: H.Q. mined Dug-out - 1 OR. to hospital. - Lieut W. J. McGill rejoins Coy. H.Q. - 1 OR. to hospital.	W.A.R.B.
	2nd.		No: 2 Section wiring - No: 4 Section wiring - No: 3 Section on Dugouts - No. 1 Section hand over dugout work for Div: H.Q. at WARLUS to 512th F. Coy. R.E. + rejoins Coy. in ARRAS. - 1 OR. wounded. - Capt. Bourne reconnoitres Battle Position in BLANGY-TRENCH.	W.A.R.B.
	3rd.		Work as yesterday continued. - Lieut Pinnock attends C.E. (XVII Corps) office to make arrangements regarding handing over of entrenchment work of FICHEAUX - Switch line to C.R.E. XVII Corps Troops. - Major Kingsford + Lieut Pinnock tape out new FICHEAUX-RESERVE line at night. Heavy enemy shelling in vicinity of billets.	W.A.R.B. W.A.R.B.
	5th.		No. 1 Section placing of concertinas in front of FICHEAUX FRONT. No 2 Section placing bombing blocks in trenches running forward from BLANGY System. - No 3 Section finish work on Dug-outs for time as instructed by C.R.E. No 4 Section cutting bays in FICHEAUX-SUPPORT (night 5th - 6th). - 3 OR. to hospital.	W.A.R.B.
	4th.		No 1 Section placing concertinas in front of FICHEAUX-FRONT LINE - No 3 Section Dug outs - Nos 2 + 4 Sections making concertinas at AGNY DUMP. - Capt Bourne re-tapes about 400 yds of FICHEAUX Reserve as instructed by C.R.E. making fire bays 24 ft long. - 2 OR. to hospital.	W.A.R.B.
	6th.		3 Sections making concertinas. - 1 Section wiring "dead" ground at M.17.a. - wiring Stores for road blocks on NEUVILLE VITASSE road at trench crossings placed on site. - 1 OR to hospital. - 2 OR. from hospital.	W.A.R.B.
	7th.		All 4 Sections on wiring of FICHEAUX-SWITCH FRONT-LINE in view of enemy attack on morning of 8th being probable. - Capt Bourne reconnoitres ARRAS Defences with C.R.E. XVII Corps Troops. - 1 OR. from hospital. 1 OR. to hospital. - 1 Infty. N.C.O. + 3 Infty. ORs. rejoin their unit from Bridge Guard. C.R.E. visits Coy. H.Q.	W.A.R.B.
	8th.		No: 2 Section making Concertinas - remaining 3 Sections wiring as last night. - Major Capt reconnoitre Battle Positions with runners. - 4 OR. Reinforcements from R.E. Base Depot.	W.A.R.B.
	9th.		Nos 1. 3. 4 Sections wiring as last night - No: 2 Section (working strength very weak) employed on "Details". - 1 OR. to hospital.	W.A.R.B.
	10th.		All Sections employed with Infantry on manufacture of Concertinas for FICHEAUX SWITCH. - billets shelled in evening - no casualties. - Lieut Macfarlane resumes command of No 3 Section. - 2nd Lieut Palmer goes to take temporary charge of Horse Lines. - 2nd Lieut Giles takes over temporary command of No 2 Section.	W.A.R.B.

(A7092). Wt. W12839/M1293. 75,0 0. 1/17. D. D. & L., Ltd. Forms/C.2118/14.

513TH (LONDON) FIELD COY., R.E.
No. ....
Date. ....

Instructions regarding War Diaries and Intelligence Summaries are contained in F. S. Regs., Part II. and the Staff Manual respectively. Title pages will be prepared in manuscript.

WAR DIARY
or
~~INTELLIGENCE SUMMARY.~~

(Erase heading not required.)

Army Form C. 2118.

Place	Date	Hour	Summary of Events and Information	Remarks and references to Appendices
	MAY.			
ARRAS.	11th		Rest Day for all Sections - Infty training carried out also Baths. - 2 OR to Hospital.	WARB.
G.27.b.15.90	12th		Coy. making Concertinas at Bull Dog Dump - 5 trees felled at S.E. Corner of TILLOY WOOD to form obstacle across sunken road - ACHICOURT BRIDGE repaired - C.R.E. + Major Kingsford go over work on wiring of TELEGRAPH HILL SWITCH	WARB.
	13th		All Sections wiring TELEGRAPH HILL SWITCH night 13th-14th - Lieut Runnock carries out demolition work on concrete O.P. at N.7.c.0.5. 2 OR report from RE Base Depot.	WARB.
	14th		All Sections wiring as last night - about 6 bombs dropped near working party by aircraft (thought to be British) - 1 OR wounded - 1 OR from hospital - 2 OR to hospital - Capt Murray R.A.M.C. makes inspection of Coy.	WARB
	15th		All Sections wiring as last night - C.R.E. visits work - 4 OR to Hospital - 1 OR from hospital - Lt Pearce proceeds on gas course.	WARB
	16th		Work as yesterday - Major G.I. KINGSFORD D.S.O. hands over Command of Coy. to Capt. Bourne until arrival of new O.C. - bridge demolition at WAGNONLIEU L 21 c 5.4 taken over from 10th R.C.R.E. -	WARB.
	17th		No 3 Section making Concertinas - Nos 1-2-4 Sections on Gas Protection & Standing by for Day work on Dugouts. - 1 OR rejoins from RE Base Depot	WARB.
	18th		No 3 Section making gaps in wire of TELEGRAPH HILL SWITCH Nos 1 and 2 Sections on dug-outs. No 4 Section on gas protection and preparing dug-out material. 2 ORs from Hospl.	H.G.P.
	19th		No 3 Section making gaps in BLANGY TRENCH wire. Nos 1, 2 and 4 Sections as 18th. 1 O.R. to Hospital, 2 ORs from Hospital	H.G.P.
	20th		Rest Day for Nos 1, 3 and 4 Sections. No 2 Section preparing dug out material. 4 ORs on repairing burst water main at M 5 d, stopped by gas shells. 3 ORs from Inf. arrive as guard for Bridge at L 21 c 5.4. Lt KIDMAN RE reconnoitres pipe line M 12 d to H 31 a.	H.G.P.
	21st		Rest Day for No 2 Sect. Nos 1 and 3 Sections on dug outs No 4 preparing material. Experimental work on Sortie steps in Telegraph Hill Switch started. 3 Tetrahedrons for survey marks made.	H.G.P.
	22nd		Nos 1, 2 + 3 Sections on dug outs. No 4 Section preparing material. Burst water main repaired in M 5 d. Tetrahedrons erected. 1 OR to hospital	H.G.P.
	23rd		Sections employed as yesterday. Tetrahedrons surveyed. Party to repair new burst in water main at night. 2 OR to hospital 2 OR from hospital. 8 O.R. from base as reinforcements 1 remaining at Transport lines for inoculation. 2 OR missing from party thro' air raid	H.G.P.

(A7092). Wt. W12839/M1293. 750,000. 1/17. D. D. & L., Ltd. Forms/C.2118/14.

Instructions regarding War Diaries and Intelligence Summaries are contained in F. S. Regs., Part II. and the Staff Manual respectively. Title pages will be prepared in manuscript.

513th (LONDON) FIELD COY., R.E.
No.........
Date.........

WAR DIARY
or
~~INTELLIGENCE SUMMARY.~~
(Erase heading not required.)

Army Form C. 2118.

Place	Date	Hour	Summary of Events and Information	Remarks and references to Appendices
ARRAS G27.b 15.90	MAY. 24th		Nos. 1 and 2 Sections on dugouts. No 4 Section preparing material and on water supply work. No 3 Section cutting trenches 3' deep across NEUVILLE VITASSE-BEAURAINS RD connecting BLANGY and BLANGY SUPPORT Trenches and bridging same. C.Q.M.S BAUMBROUGH proceeds to ENGLAND to attend Cadet Course. 1 OR to Hospital	H.G.P.
	25th		Nos 1 and 2 Sections on dugouts. No 3. on reconnaissance of CTs in TELEGRAPH HILL SYSTEM. and Water Supply. No 4 preparing dug out material, making trench mortar baseplates and on Water Supply 1. OR to Hospital. 1 OR rejoins from CRE office	H.G.P.
	26th		Nos 1 + 2 and part No 3. Sect. on dug-outs. (latter party hindered by shell fire). Part No 3 on water supply. No 4 Sect. on preparing dug out material and water supply. 3 OR arrive from Base as reinforcements. 1 OR rejoins from Gas Course 1 OR rejoins from CRINCHON BRIDGE.	H.G.P.
	27th		Work as yesterday. CRE inspects horses and vehicles with O.C. at WAGNONLIEU 1. OR rejoins from hospital	H.G.P.
	28th		Work as yesterday. 8 O.Rs connecting BLANGY TRENCH across ARRAS-WANCOURT RD. Short nights work owing to our raid. 1 OR rejoins from Transport Lines after inoculation. 1 OR to Hospital	H.G.P.
	29th		Rest Day for all except those on water supply and R.A. work	H.G.P.
	30th		Nos 1 and 2 Sections on dugouts. No 3. on dugouts and water supply. No. 4 preparing dug out material and on water supply. 6 OR extra supplied for R.A work. 1. OR wounded. 1. OR to Hospital. M.O. inspects billets and kitchens	H.G.P.
	31st		Work as yesterday.	H.G.P.

W.G.R. Bourne
Captain, R.E.
O.C. 513 Field Co.

(A7092). Wt. W12839/M1293. 750,000. 1/17. D. D. & L., Ltd. Forms/C.2118/14.

Instructions regarding War Diaries and Intelligence Summaries are contained in F. S. Regs., Part II. and the Staff Manual respectively. Title pages will be prepared in manuscript.

WAR DIARY
or
~~INTELLIGENCE SUMMARY.~~
(Erase heading not required.)

513 Fd Coy RE
Vol 28

Army Form C. 2118.

Place	Date	Hour	Summary of Events and Information	Remarks and references to Appendices
ARRAS. G27b.15.90.	JUNE 1st.		Nos 1 and 2 sections on dug out work. No 3 on dug outs and water supply. No. 4 Section preparing dug out material and on water supply. Lieut Macfarlane RE appointed O/C Brigade working parties. 1. OR to Hospital. Sergt Cook Instr. spends day with Coy. Cooks	H.G.P.
	2nd		Work as yesterday. Gas alarm at 3.30 am. (slight). 1. OR reports forward from Transport lines. 2 OR to Hospital	H.G.P.
	3rd		Work as yesterday. 1. OR from Base as Reinforcement. 1. OR from Hospital. 1. OR to Hospital	H.G.P.
	4th		Work as yesterday. 2 OR sent to assist L.R.B in tree felling on CAMBRAI RD.	H.G.P.
	5th		38 men from different sections on Shooting Range, remainder of Coy. employed as yesterday. 1. OR departs on Gas Course. 1. OR attends demonstration by 1st Army Catering Instructor. 1. OR from Hospital	H.G.P.
	6th.		No. 1. Section on dug outs. No. 2 dug outs and trench maintenance. No 3 and 4 on trench maintenance and water supply. Water pumped thro' to CAMBRAI RD.	H.G.P.
	7th		Company rest day.	H.G.P.
	8th		43 O.Rs shooting on range. Remainder of Coy. employed as yesterday. Inf guards on bridges prepared for demolition relieved. 5. OR from Base as reinforcements. No 2 Section left at 7 pm for 3 days rest at WAGNONLIEU. 1. OR joins from 247. Empt. Coy. replacing Pte Murdoch	H.G.P.
	9th.		No. 1. Section on dugouts. No 3 on work in line for Brigade, No 4 on water supply. 1. OR rejoins from Gas Course.	H.G.P.

Instructions regarding War Diaries and Intelligence Summaries are contained in F. S. Regs., Part II. and the Staff Manual respectively. Title pages will be prepared in manuscript.

WAR DIARY

~~or~~

~~INTELLIGENCE SUMMARY.~~

(Erase heading not required.)

Army Form C. 2118.

Place	Date	Hour	Summary of Events and Information	Remarks and references to Appendices
ARRAS G27b 15.90.	JUNE 10th		No1. Section on Dugouts in line. No 3. Section on Brigade work in line. No 4. Section on Water supply. Lieut Pinnock attached to C.R.E. for period.	[initials]
	11th		Work as yesterday. 5 O.R. innoculated. 1.3 + 4 Sections test Gas helmets thro. Gas Room. 1 OR to Hospital.	[initials]
	12th		Work as yesterday. No 2. move to forward billets from short period of rest at Transport lines. II Lieut Palmer moves to forward billets. II Lieut Kidman goes to Transport lines i/c Transport + HQ details. No 4. Section moves to Transport lines for 3 days rest. No 2 Section work during afternoon at RE dump making concertinas. 5 OR innoculated.	[initials]
	13th		No 1 Section working on Dugouts, No 2 Section on night work, cutting gaps in wire. No 3 Section on Brigade work in line both at day + night. 4 O.R. to Hospital. Lieut Palmer out with No 2 Section. 4 OR innoculated	[initials]
	14th		Work as yesterday 5 OR innoculated. 2 O.R. from Hospital.	[initials]
	15th		Work as yesterday. 5 OR. innoculated 1 OR to Hospital.	[initials]
	16th		Part Rest day, but a few men working to supervise infantry parties. Lieut Pinnock leaves the company + goes to 282 Army Troops Company. Lieut MacSwiney reports here for duty in exchange. 1 OR rejoins from leave. St Giles and No 1 Section go to wagon lines for 3 days rest. No 4 Section returns to Arras for work.	[initials]

(A7092). Wt W12839/M1293. 75,000. 1/17. D. D. & L., Ltd. Forms/C.2118/14.

Instructions regarding War Diaries and Intelligence Summaries are contained in F. S. Regs., Part II. and the Staff Manual respectively. Title pages will be prepared in manuscript.

WAR DIARY
or
~~INTELLIGENCE SUMMARY.~~
(Erase heading not required.)

Army Form C. 2118.

Place	Date	Hour	Summary of Events and Information	Remarks and references to Appendices
ARRAS G27b15.90	1918 June 17th		No.1 Section at Wagon lines resting. No2 Section making [illegible] at Bulldog Dump. No3 Section working on [illegible] Trench improvement jobs for Bde. Capt Bourne takes Lieut Macswiney around the line. No 4 Section Lt Macswiney in Command is employed on Dugouts in the forward area. 7 O.R. reinforcements from Base Depot. 2 O.R. from Hospital. 57 O.R. innoculated.	McM.
	18th		No.2. Sections continue on cutting gaps in wire night work. No3 Sections working with No 4 on Dugouts. 7 O.R. innoculated 1 O.R. to Hospital.	McM.
	19th		Capt Bourne goes round line with CRE to select sites etc for new Dugouts, large new Dugout scheme about to be started. No 4 + 3 Sections continue on Dugouts in hand No.2. Sections go to shooting practice in afternoon. ~~Sergt Welsh~~ 1 O.R. from Hospital 2 O.R. to Hospital.	McM.
	20th		No1. Section returns to forward billets from period of rest at Wagon lines Lt Giles also returns to forward billets. No 2. Section under Lt Palmer commence new Dugouts. No.3 Section salving material + move to Wagon lines for period of rest at 6. pm No 4 Section under Lt Macswiney continue on Dugouts in Rallying points. Sergt Welsh to Base Depot.	McM.
	21st.		No1 Section 2 + 4 also Dugouts 3 shifts per day. On new dugout scheme 1 O.R. sent to assist infantry in cutting across road + placing bridge.	McM.
	22nd		Section work as yesterday. 1 O.R. sent to London Scottish H.Q to assist on Gas curtains. O.C. visits Transport lines for inspection. Burst in water pipe repaired during night.	McM.

(A7092). Wt. W12839/M1293. 75 ,0 0. 1/17. D. D. & L., Ltd. Forms/C.2118/14.

WAR DIARY
or
~~INTELLIGENCE SUMMARY.~~
(Erase heading not required.)

Instructions regarding War Diaries and Intelligence Summaries are contained in F. S. Regs., Part II. and the Staff Manual respectively. Title pages will be prepared in manuscript.

Army Form C. 2118.

Place	Date	Hour	Summary of Events and Information	Remarks and references to Appendices
ARRAS G27b15.90	1918 June 23rd		Sections work as yesterday. Capt. Bourne goes around the jobs in the line with Brigade General.	[illegible]
	24th		Rest day. Sections undergo Infantry training for 1 hour including Rifle + Gas helmet inspection. Work on water line continues. No. 3 Section returns to forward billets for rest at wagon lines. No 2. Section moves to wagon lines for period of 7 days rest + work on horselines + wagons etc. 2 OR return from work at D.H.Q. 2 OR reinforcements (Sappers) 1 OR to Hospital, 1 OR from Hospital	[illegible]
	25th		No. 1 Section continues work on Rally point dugouts. No 3. Section takes over No 2 Sections work, making new Batt H.Q. Dugouts. No 4 Section continues on reclaiming old Dug outs at Rallying pts.	[illegible]
	26th		Work as yesterday. [illegible] observe today as a "Rest day." 30 O.R. shoot practices 3 + 4 on Rifle Range. 12 OR innoculated. Guard on Bridges changed this morning. 3 O.R. mounted Section to Hospital.	[illegible]
	27th		Work on Dugouts as yesterday. 1 OR. from Hospital.	
	28th		Work as yesterday. No. 3. Section constructing infantry O.P.s. in a near front line. 8 O.R. to Hospital. 9 O.R. (drivers) reinforcements from Base Depot.	[illegible]
	29th		Work as yesterday on Dugouts, new M.G.E. commenced by No 3 Section. 12 O.R. Shoot practices 5 + 6 on Rifle range. 5 O.R. to Hospital. (fever) 30 OR. of Resting Section and details go to Dumb Bells at [illegible].	[illegible]
	30th		Work as yesterday. 1 O.R. from Hospital. 2 OR to Hospital. (fever)	[illegible]

W.A.R. Bourne.
Captain, R.E.
for O.C. [illegible] Field Co.

(A7092). Wt. W12839/M1293. 75,0.0. 1/17. D. D. & L., Ltd. Forms/C.2118/14.

6

Instructions regarding War Diaries and Intelligence Summaries are contained in F. S. Regs., Part II. and the Staff Manual respectively. Title pages will be prepared in manuscript.

WAR DIARY
or
~~INTELLIGENCE SUMMARY.~~
(Erase heading not required.)

513 Fd Coy RE

Army Form C. 2118.

Vol 29

Place	Date 1918	Hour	Summary of Events and Information	Remarks and references to Appendices
ARRAS G27b15.90.	July 1st.		1 Section continues on reclaiming dugouts. No 3. on new Batt. H.Q. Dugouts & M.G.E. No 4 section reclaiming & making new dugouts. Major D.H. Steers RE takes over command of Company	[initials]
	2nd		Work as yesterday. 6 O.R. to Hospital.	[initials]
	3rd		Work as yesterday. 4 O.R. to Hospital.	[initials]
	4th.		~~Work as yesterday~~ Company Rest day. 4 O.R. to Hospital (fever) 2 O.R. from Hospital.	[initials]
	~~5th.~~		No. 2 Section return from period of rest at Wagon lines, No 4 Section go to Wagon line for rest period.	
	5th.		No 1 Section continue with work reclaiming dugouts & building concrete O.P. No. 2. Section take over work left by No 4 section under Lieut Lucas reclaiming dugouts in Rallying posts. No 3 Section continue on new dugouts for Batt H.Q. Aid Post & MGE under Lieut Palmer. 3 O.R. to hospital 5 O.R. from Hospital.	[initials]
	6th.		Work as yesterday. 4 O.R to hospital 2 O.R from Hospital.	[initials]
	7th.		Work as yesterday. Capt Browne proceeds to England on leave. Sergt Brown goes for course at RE School Rouen. 3 O.R. to Hospital. 11 O.R from Hospital	[initials]
	8th.		Work as yesterday. No. 2. Section finish one Dugout & assist No. 3. section on Batt H.Q. 6 O.R. employed at RE Dumps preparing material. 3 O.R. to Hospital. 7 O.R from Hospital. 1 O.R wounded.	[initials]

(A7092) Wt W12839/M1293 750,000 1/17 D. D. & L., Ltd. Forms/C.2118/14.

Instructions regarding War Diaries and Intelligence Summaries are contained in F. S. Regs., Part II. and the Staff Manual respectively. Title pages will be prepared in manuscript.

WAR DIARY

~~or~~

~~INTELLIGENCE SUMMARY.~~

(Erase heading not required.)

Army Form C. 2118.

Place	Date	Hour	Summary of Events and Information	Remarks and references to Appendices
ARRAS G27b15.90.	1918 JULY 9th.		No 1 Section continues work on reclaiming dugouts. and building concrete O.P. No 2 Section continue on dugouts in Rallying pts. No 3 Section on Batt H.Q. Aid Post & M.G.E. Dugouts in reserve line. All sections working 3 - 6 hour shifts with infantry working parties. 9 O.R. from Hospital 1. O.R. to hospital. Difficulty in getting up material last night, owing to hostile shell fire after relief by us.	[initials]
	10th		Work as yesterday. 1 OR. to hospital. 8 O.R. from Hospital.	[initials]
	11th.		Work as yesterday. Several infantry working parties are withdrawn owing to relief. One officer and 40 R. of 2nd Canadian Div. C.E. report at 3.30 pm to take over work. 5 OR from Hospital.	[initials]
	12th.		Work as yesterday. Attached Pioneers withdrawn to-day, owing to relief. 6 O.R. from Hospital. Bridge Guards relieved by Guards from 2nd Canadian Div.	[initials]
	13th.		Work as yesterday, but to knock off at end of 2nd shift i.e. 10.30 pm. No 1 & 2 Toolcarts are taken back to Transport lines to-day. 5 O.R. from Hospital. 1 OR to Hospital.	[initials]
	14th.		Move to Wagnonlieu at 2.0 pm. Billets at Arras handed over to Billet Wardens. Whole Company billetted at Wagnonlieu for night. 3 OR. to Hospital.	[initials]
WAGNONLIEU Sheet 51C. L21d.9.6.	15th.		Transport move off to join Brigade column at Agny les Duisans at 7-am. Dismounted Section less cyclists Entrain at DAINVILLE. and arrive DIEVAL 4.30 pm march to.	[initials]

(A7092). Wt W12839/M1293 75 ,6.0. 1/17. D. D. & L., Ltd. Forms/C.2118/14.

Army Form C. 2118.

Instructions regarding War Diaries and Intelligence Summaries are contained in F. S. Regs., Part II. and the Staff Manual respectively. Title pages will be prepared in manuscript.

WAR DIARY
or
~~INTELLIGENCE SUMMARY.~~
(Erase heading not required.)

Place	Date	Hour	Summary of Events and Information	Remarks and references to Appendices
	1918			
BEUGIN	July 15	cont.	Beugin. arrive Beugin 5.30 pm. Mounted portions arrive Beugin at 3.30 pm. Billets here not very good, rather crowded. 1 O.R. to	WM.
P.7 a.5.5. Sheet No. 44B.	16.		Observed as a Rest day, to allow sections etc to make cook houses + improve billets. Parade for Rifle + Gas helmet drill at 9.30 am. 1 O.R. Instructor attached for training. Bombing + Bayonet fighting. 2 O.R. to Hospital.	WM.
	17.		First day of Training programme carried out. All dismounted men practise on rifle Range 100ˣ + 200ˣ. Three hours of infantry training also carried out, including Bayonet fighting, Bombing, Open order Battle drill. 1 O.R. to Hospital. 4 O.R. from Hospital. 1 O.R. reinforcement. Orders received to move to BAJUS. II Lieut goes to arrange billets at 3.30 pm.	WM.
BAJUS O.22 b 1.1. Sheet 44B.	18.		Company moves off at 9.45 am, arrives at BAJUS 11.30 am. Lewis Gunners continue with training from 2 pm to 4 pm. Remainder of Sections work on improving Billets etc.	WM.
	19.		All sections + mounted section training in Lewis Gun. Battle order Drill. Physical Training. Bombing + Bayonet fighting. Company draw Bridging equipment for training purposes. Under orders to be ready to move in 4 hours, by Bus or ~~Strategical~~ Strategical Train. 1 O.R. to Hospital. 2 O.R. from from Hospital. 1 Infantry Officer + 2 N.C.O.s attached to help with training.	WM.
	20.		Training as yesterday continues. 1 O.R. to Hospital.	WM.
	21.		Training in Pontooning Bridging, Lewis Gun + Close Order Drill. 5 O.R. from Hospital.	
	22nd.		Training in Lewis Gun, drill, Bayonet fighting, + Open order Battledrill. To 1st Army Rest Camp II Lt Giles 7 O.R. 4 O.R. to Hospital	WM.

(A7092) Wt. W12839/M1293. 75,000. 1/17. D. D. & L., Ltd. Forms/C.2118/14.

Instructions regarding War Diaries and Intelligence Summaries are contained in F. S. Regs., Part II. and the Staff Manual respectively. Title pages will be prepared in manuscript.

WAR DIARY
or
~~INTELLIGENCE SUMMARY.~~
(Erase heading not required.)

Army Form C. 2118.

Place	Date	Hour	Summary of Events and Information	Remarks and references to Appendices
BAJUS O226 1.1. Sheet 44B.	1918 July 23rd		1,2,3 + 4 Sections less 8 men per Section Pontoon Training at Pond at O12 central 8 men per section continue with Lewis Gun Instruction. 1 O.R. to Hospital 2 O.R. from Hospital. II Lieut McGill is acting Adjutant to CRE, while Capt Orr is on leave	MM.
	24th		Sections training in P.T. Close order Drill, Hasty Demolitions, Bombing & Bayonet fighting. Lewis Gunners continue. Capt Bourne returns from leave to U.K. 1 O.R. to hospital.	MM.
	25th		Sections Pontooning, Lewis Gun Instruction continues 1 O.R. to Hospital 2 O.R. from Hospital.	MM.
	26th		Training continues as on 24th. Musketry on Range is started in afternoon 1 O.R. from Hospital.	MM
	27th		Company now only at 4 hours notice to move only between the hours of 3 + 7 am. Otherwise at 24 hours notice. The day is devoted to running off heats etc for R.E. Sports. at the Quarry O12 central. 1 O.R. from Hospital.	MM.
	28th		No Training or Work - Heats for 56th Divisional R.E. Sports held. 3 OR. rejoin Unit from hospital	W.A.R.B.
	29th		Do: Do: - 56th Div. R.E. Sports held - receive orders from 169th Infty Brigade to move to CAMBLIGNEUL on 30th inst. - II Lieut K Palmer + party proceed billeting - 1. OR to hospital	W.A.R.B.
	30th		Company moves to CAMBLIGNEUL by road - II Lieut. A V Kidman, acting on instructions from C.R.E. collects Pontoons & Bridging Stores from Training Ground & hands same with Army Park. O.C. goes with C.R.E. to ARRAS to see Canadian R.E. prior to taking over.	W.A.R.B.
CAMBLIGNEUL W.14.d.	31st		Coy. does no Training. O.C. Lieuts MacSwiney, Macfarlane, Kidman & Palmer go to ARRAS to go round work with Officers of 2nd C.E. Batt. - Lieuts. Macfarlane, Kidman & Palmer remain in ARRAS. Officer of 512th Fld. Coy temporarily attached.	W.A.R.B.

W.A.R. Bourne
Captain, R.E.
for O.C. 513 Field Co.

Instructions regarding War Diaries and Intelligence Summaries are contained in F. S. Regs., Part II. and the Staff Manual respectively. Title pages will be prepared in manuscript.

WAR DIARY
or
~~INTELLIGENCE SUMMARY~~.
(Erase heading not required.)

513 (LONDON) FIELD COY., R.E.
No .... Date ....

Vol 30

Army Form C. 2118.

Place	Date	Hour	Summary of Events and Information	Remarks and references to Appendices
CAMBLIGNEUL	AUGUST 1.		Enemy bombing district - Coy. moves to ARRAS. Sappers by light Railway under O.C. - Transport under Capt. Bourne by road to WAGNONLIEU - work taken over from 2nd Canadian Engineer Batt. - Lieut MacSwiney takes over command of Horse lines.	WARB
W.14.d. ARRAS G.27.b.15.90	2.		Work on dug-outs (under 169th Infty Bde) commenced - C.R.E. visits O.C. - Lieut Kidman hands over Water Supply work to R.E. Officer of 57th Division - O.C. attends Conference called by C.R.E. & visits Brigade, but is unable to get definite instructions for starting work to-morrow. II LIEUT. K. PALMER from London R. to be Sec Lt. prec. July 21st 1917 (Aug. 1st). 4 Section working under orders from 169th Infty. Bde.	WARB.
	3.		Work on dug-outs continued with - O.C. shows Capt Johnson of 1/5th Cheshires work that his Coy is to take in hand - 1 O.R. to hospital.	WARB.
	4.		Work as yesterday - Nos 1-2 & part 4 Sections under II Lieut Palmer on Dugouts, M.G. Emplacement & O.Post - No 3. Section working with Support Batt. (L.R.B.) on repair & maintenance of C.T.s under Lieut Macfarlane - remainder of No 4. Section work on Water Supply under II Lieut Kidman - "A" Coy. 1/5th Cheshires on reclaiming trenches in M.18.b. under orders of O.C. 513th F. Coy RE. - 20 O.R. from M.G. Batt. attached for work on Emplacement - 1 O.R. to U.K. on leave - 7 O.R.s attached for rations i/c of Baths at WAGNONLIEU. - 8 O.R. Infty Bridge Guards for GRINCHON & WAGNONLIEU Bridges.	W.ARB.
	5.		Work as yesterday - 1 O.R. rejoins from Lewis Gun Course - 1 O.R. rejoins from R.E. School Rouen - 1 O.R. proceeds to R.E. School - ROUEN -	WARB.
	6.		Work as yesterday - great difficulty in obtaining R.E. material from C.R.E.	WARB.
	7.		Work as yesterday - II LIEUT. GILES. RE. + 7. O.R.s rejoin from Rest Camps - O.C. experiments with Camouflet Charges for Dug-outs	WARB
	8		Work as yesterday - II Lieut Giles takes over part of dugouts from II Lieut. K. Palmer - No 3. Section working on shelters for Rt. Batt. H.Q. in addition to work as above. - "A" Coy. Cheshires - U Baying INTERMEDIATE LINE also deepening & clearing	WARB.
	9.		Work as yesterday - Capt Bourne & Lieut MacSwiney visit site of new Horse Lines at WARLUS. with C.R.E. - 1 O.R. attached to M.O. for training in First Aid - 1 O.R. to hospital.	WARB.
	10.		Work as yesterday - R.E. material still very hard to obtain - Div. Engineers eliminating Show. 513th Pontoon Wagon placed for Army Horse Show. II LIEUT. A.V. KIDMAN. R.E. promoted Lieut. (July 15.) 1918.	WARB.
	11.		Work on dugouts, shelters & Water Supply continued with - Horse Lines move to No 1. Camp WARLUS. - O.C. experiments with Camouflet charges for dugout work with success.	WARB.
	12.		Work as yesterday - 1 O.R. Leave to U.K. - 4 O.R. attached for Water Patrol Duties	WARB.

(A7092). Wt. W12839/M1293. 75,0.0. 1/17. D. D. & L., Ltd. Forms/C.2118/14.

SHEET. 51.C.

Instructions regarding War Diaries and Intelligence Summaries are contained in F. S. Regs., Part II. and the Staff Manual respectively. Title pages will be prepared in manuscript.

WAR DIARY
or
~~INTELLIGENCE SUMMARY~~.
(Erase heading not required.)

513TH (LONDON) FIELD COY., R.E.

No .... Date ....

Army Form C. 2118.

Place	Date	Hour	Summary of Events and Information	Remarks and references to Appendices
ARRAS. G.27.b.15.90.	AUGUST 13.		Work as yesterday – Capt Bourne visits Horse lines at WARLUS – 2 OR report from R.E. Base Depot – ~~4 OR attached for Water Patrol Duties~~ 1 OR. to Hospital.	W.A.R.B.
	14.		Rest Day for all dismounted men, with exception of those working on M.G. Emplacement – Warning Order from 169th Infty Brigade as to Divisional Relief – 1 OR. to Hospital.	W.A.R.B.
	15.		Work on dugouts resumed – 1 L/C (Alfd Friend) joins from Base Depot – 2 ORs rejoin from Hospital.	W.A.R.B.
	16.		Transport Mounted Section under Capt. Bourne move, by road, to DENIER; all work in forward area handed over to 73rd Field Coy. R.E. including Bridge & Dump Demolitions – Lieut MacSwiney R.E. proceeds to 1st Army Infantry Course. II Lieut McGill remains as a/Adjut to CRE 56th Division v/c of Capt ORR'S indisposition. – 20 Machine Gunners rejoin their Unit also Bridge Guards & Water Patrol – 1 OR to Hospital.	W.A.R.B.
	17.		Dismounted portion of Coy move to DENIER by Train.	W.A.R.B.
DENIER. I.19.a.8.0.	18.		Training carried out. Sapper GRAHAM awarded Field Punishment & sent to 1/5th Cheshire Pioneer Batt for disposal. 1 OR. rejoined from Hospital.	W.A.R.B.
	19.		Dismounted Portion of Coy. move to ARRAS by Bus under orders of 169th Infty. Bde. – Transport move by road to DUISSANS. – Lieut KIRMAN proceeds U.K. on leave.	W.A.R.B.
ARRAS.	20.		Company moves by road to FOSSEUX night 20th 21st, under orders 169th Infty. Bde.	W.A.R.B.
FOSSEUX.	21.		Company " " " SAULTY " 21st 22nd " " " "	W.A.R.B.
SAULTY. V.2.a.	22.		Company stands by to move at 1 hours notice – II LIEUT. PALMER attached temporarily to 512th Fld. Coy to act as liason Officer. – II LIEUT. GILES goes forward to reconnoitre Battle Positions with Officers of 169th Infty Bde. Sapper GRAHAM returns.	W.A.R.B.
BAILLEULVAL	23.		Company moves by road to BAILLEULVAL – bivouacs for 5 hrs in field. – 1 OR. rejoins from Hospital. – 1 OR. reports from R.E. Base Depot.	W.A.R.B.
W.3.b.	24.		Company moves to approx. X.4 central & in afternoon H.Q. Sappers move forward to BOISIEUX-AU-MONT on Water Supply – Mounted Section spend night at BALMONT MILL under Capt. Bourne. – Enemy night bombing. II LIEUT. K. PALMER rejoins from 512th Fld. Coy. R.E.	W.A.R.B.

(A7092). Wt. W12839/M1293. 750,000. 1/17. D. D. & L., Ltd. Forms/C.2118/14.

Instructions regarding War Diaries and Intelligence Summaries are contained in F. S. Regs., Part II. and the Staff Manual respectively. Title pages will be prepared in manuscript.

WAR DIARY

or

~~INTELLIGENCE SUMMARY.~~

(Erase heading not required.)

513TH (LONDON) FIELD COY., R.E.

No. .... Date ....

Army Form C. 2118.

Place	Date	Hour	Summary of Events and Information	Remarks and references to Appendices
BOISEUX-AU-MONT. S.9.d.9.3.	AUGUST 25		Company employed on sinking wells 12'0" × 12'0" in bed of COJEUL RIVER (dry) at S.15.b. - Horse watering troughs being erected at points along COJEUL between & in villages of BOISEUX-AU-MONT & BOISEUX-ST-MARC - Capt. Bourne with mounted Section & H.Q. Details rejoin Coy. H.Q. Pioneers assist in well sinking.	W.A.R.B.
	26.		Coy. employed as yesterday - 2 Water Cart filling points established in BOISEUX-AU-MONT - 2 OR.s to Hospital.	W.A.R.B.
	27.		Coy. still on Water Supply working at high pressure - Bath House for use of Infantry put in hand - great difficulty in obtaining Water Supply tools especially Stocks & dies (gas thread) which is delaying work considerably. Shortage of Pumps & Hose. - 1 OR. to Hospital. C.R.E. visits Coy. H.Q.	W.A.R.B.
	28.		Water Points being completed - CROISILLES taken. II Lieut Palmer & N.C.O.s at once go forward on Water Reconnaissance - Bath House nearing completion - 2nd Cpl. PALMER rejoins after attending Horse management Course.	W.A.R.B.
	29.		Improvement to Water Points - repair & maintenance of Pumps - Bath House erection & fitting of Heating Apparatus - II Lieut K. Palmer returns from Water Reconnaissance & goes forward with No. 2 Section & Bivouacs at approx T.22.a. - he sinks two shafts at T.18.b.6.2. in order to find water for horses. 3 OR to Hospital.	W.A.R.B.
	30.		Water Supply work as yesterday - Bath House at BOISIEUX-AU-MONT completed - new Bath House at BOIRY-BECQUERELLE commenced - II Lieut Giles [?] relieves II Lieut Palmer & takes over well sinking & preparation for Horse Watering Points in SENSEE RIVER - 1 OR. to hospital - 1 OR. leave to U.K. - enemy night bombing near by Coy. billets	W.A.R.B.
	31.		Divisional Relief by 52nd Div. - 413th Fld Coy. take over all Watering Points - 412th Fld. Coy. take over work in SENSEE River. II Lieut Giles [?] & No: 2 Section return to Coy. H.Q. - Bath House being worked on at full pressure. - 1 OR. to hospital.	W.A.R.B.

W.A.R. Bourne
Captain, R.E.
for O.C. 513 F[?] [?]

(A7092). Wt. W12839/M1293. 75,0.0. 1/17. D. D. & L., Ltd. Forms/C.2118/14.

Instructions regarding War Diaries and Intelligence Summaries are contained in F. S. Regs., Part II. and the Staff Manual respectively. Title pages will be prepared in manuscript.

WAR DIARY
or
~~INTELLIGENCE SUMMARY.~~
(Erase heading not required.)

513

513TH (LONDON) FIELD COY., R.E.

Army Form C. 2118.

2-10-18

3/

Place	Date	Hour	Summary of Events and Information	Remarks and references to Appendices
BOISEUX-AU-MONT. 59 d 9.3.	SEPTEMBER 1.		Company employed on erection of new Bath House at BOIRY-BECQUERELLE - withdrawing Lift Force Pumps from Watering Points handed over to 52nd Division & repairing same - Splinter-proofing bivouacs & Camp improvements - making water troughs etc for Divisional Mobile Water Supply Stores - final handing over of Water Supply work to 413th Field Coy. - 1 OR. re-engagement leave to U.K. - 1 OR. to be temporarily attached to C.R.E. Aid Post for instruction - 1 OR. to hospital. Enemy night bombing.	WARB.
	2.		Bath House completed - experimental well sunk in COJEUL - water troughs manufactured & portable Bath House & other water supply stores being prepared for mobile column - L.F. pumps withdrawn from Watering Points overhauled - orders received from C.R.E. in afternoon to take over again Horse Watering Points from 413th Fld Coy. - 1 OR. to hospital.	WARB.
	3.		Coy. still employed on Water Supply - Lift Force Pumps together with 6 ORs. returned to 416th Fld. Coy. RE.	WARB.
	4.		Company employed on maintenance of Watering Points - preparation of Stores Equipment for Div: Mobile Water Supply Column - 1 OR. rejoins from R.E. Course ROUEN - 2 OR. from hospital.	WARB.
	5.		As yesterday - order & consequent preparations to move forward to relieve 52nd Division cancelled - 1 OR. rejoins from hospital - 1 OR. to Base Depot for medical reclassification.	WARB.
	6		Portable Bath House completed - also water troughs etc. - 1 OR. to R.E. Course. ROUEN - orders to relieve 1st Div: to move up to do so at 5.30 pm tomorrow.	WARB.
O 8 d 4.2.	7.		Company preparing to move, hand over water stores to Corps. Div. Mobile Water Supp plant to be moved by lorry. Company moves off at 5 pm to join Bde Column at BOISEUX ST MARC. 1 OR to hospital. 11 O.R. to Lewis Gun Course (Corps). II Lt Palmer goes on leave to U.K. sailing 9th. Company arrives O 8 d 4.2. and takes over billets from 512 F. Coy. RE	[illegible]

(A7092). Wt. W12839/M1293. 750,000. 1/17. D. D. & L., Ltd. Forms/C.2118/14.

Instructions regarding War Diaries and Intelligence Summaries are contained in F. S. Regs., Part II. and the Staff Manual respectively. Title pages will be prepared in manuscript.

WAR DIARY
or
~~INTELLIGENCE SUMMARY.~~
(Erase heading not required.)

513TH (LONDON) FIELD COY., R.E.
No. ......
Date ......

Army Form C. 2118.

Place	Date	Hour	Summary of Events and Information	Remarks and references to Appendices
Sheet 51B SW. 08d42.	1918 Sept. 8th		Capt Bowne goes forward to take over from 23rd Field Coy. RE. O.C. Company goes on reconnaissance with B.G.C. Company hands over to 416 F. Coy RE Billets + all water stores. Company moves to REMY O18c (central) at 3pm.	
REMY. O18c 5.5.		4.45 pm	arrive at 4.45 pm. Pontoons are returned to company by mechanical transport. Major Steers goes on leave to U.K. Capt Bowne takes over command of Company. 1 O.R. from Hospital. 1 OR to Hospital.	M.M.
	9th.		Company starts work on Bde H.Q. (169) building cut + cover shelters. 2/Lt Leslie from 512 Field Coy. is attached for duty ~~for~~ temporarily. 1 OR. returned from leave.	M.M.
	10th		Work as yesterday also 168 Bde + Batt. H.Qs and collecting timber from German Hutments + dumps. Big reconnaissance scheme has to be started tonight Lt Giles on this work. 2 OR to Hospital.	M.M.
	11th.		Work continued as yesterday. Lt Giles + 3 O.R. make reconnaissance of SENSEE MARSHES. 1 O.R. to Hospital.	M.M.
	12th.		Work on Bde + Batt H.Qs continues. Lt Giles continues with reconnaissance work. Lieut Kidman rejoins from leave to U.K.	M.M.
	13th		Work ~~—~~ as yesterday. Lt Macfarlane makes reconnaissance of part of SENSEE VALLEY. Also Lt Kidman is employed on ~~this~~ work. II Lt Giles goes to live at Batt H.Q. Left Sector in order to go out with patrols. 1 OR to Hosp.	M.M.

(A7092). Wt. W12839/M1293. 75,000. 1/17. D. D. & L., Ltd. Forms/C.2118/14.

Instructions regarding War Diaries and Intelligence Summaries are contained in F. S. Regs., Part II. and the Staff Manual respectively. Title pages will be prepared in manuscript.

WAR DIARY
or
~~INTELLIGENCE SUMMARY.~~
(Erase heading not required.)

513TH (LONDON) FIELD COY., R.E.

Army Form C. 2118.

Place	Date 1918.	Hour	Summary of Events and Information	Remarks and references to Appendices
REMY Sheet 51B SW O18 c.5.5	14-9		Company employed on Bde + Batt HQs + general accommodation. Capt Bourne + Lieut Kidman go out on a tour of Batt HQs. (II Lt Giles) 1 NCO. + small party go out in Bertham Boat to reconnoitre lakes + marshes in SENSEE VALLEY.	M.M.
	15th.		General work as yesterday. Lt Kidman continues on Left sector reconnaissance II Lt Giles on Right. Capt Bourne also goes up on reconnaissance work. 1 O.R. to 1st Aid Course at R.E.H.Q. 2 O.R. to Hospital. 1 O.R. from Hospital. C.S.M. to leave to U.K.	M.M.
	16th.		Work as yesterday. II Lieut Giles continues at Batt H.Q. 1 O.R. leave to U.K.	M.M.
	17th		Work as yesterday. Capt Bourne + II Lt Giles carry out important reconnaissance by Daylight of part of SENSEE VALLEY. 3 O.R. to Hospital.	M.M.
	18th.		Company Rest day.	M.M.
	19th.		Company preparing to move Bde work continues, + work on new H.Q. started take over front from 8th Batt C.E. 1 O.R. returned from leave U.K.	M.M.
Sheet 51B SE. P.32 d 4 5.	20th		Company less mounted section + horselines move to new Billets at P.32 d 4 5. Lt Kidman + II Lt Leslie make reconnaissance of new front. 2 O.R. to Hospital	M.M.
	21st.		Two Sections employed on Bde, Batt. + Dressing Station accommodation. remainder of company on reconnaissances + guiding + loading wagons for forward R.E. Dumps. Capt Bourne tapes out cross country track at night.	
	22nd.		Work as yesterday. Several forward Dumps were made last night + continuing to-night.	M.M.
	23rd.		Work continues as yesterday. 1 O.R. to Hosp. 3 O.R. joined as reinforcements. 1 O.R. rejoins from 1st Army Infy School. Lieut MacSwiney rejoins from 1st Army Sch.	M.M.
	24th.		Work as yesterday. remainder of Company guiding, loading + unloading wagons of R.E. material to forward dumps. 18 O.R. attached for work from 512 F.C. R.E	M.M.

(A7092) Wt. W12839/M1293. 75,000. 1/17. D. D. & L., Ltd. Forms/C.2118/14.

Instructions regarding War Diaries and Intelligence Summaries are contained in F. S. Regs., Part II. and the Staff Manual respectively. Title pages will be prepared in manuscript.

WAR DIARY
or
~~INTELLIGENCE SUMMARY.~~
(Erase heading not required.)

Army Form C. 2118.

513TH (LONDON) FIELD COY., R.E.

Place	Date 1918	Hour	Summary of Events and Information	Remarks and references to Appendices
SHEET 51B SE	Sept. 24th		2 O.R. to Hospital. 1 O.R. rejoins as reinforcement.	Initials
P32d4.5.	25th		Two sections continue work on Bde. Batt. H.Q.s. and Dressing Station remainder of Sappers on reconnaissances + carting RE stores forward. II Lt K. Palmer rejoins from leave in U.K. Major Steers rejoins from leave in UK.	Initials
	26th		All men possible rest but approx half the coy still working on Bde. H.Q. & Dressing Station - final orders & preparations made for to-morrow - remaining stores taken forward at night. 1 O.R. returns from M.O.s Aid Post.	
	27th		Active operations commence - Lieut A.V. KIDMAN & party goes forward early to reconnoitre wood & canal at W.9.a. for Infantry crossings - Major STEERS - LIEUTs MACSWINEY & GILES go forward early with Sappers & establish Coy H.Q. at BARALLE W.8.c.2.1. - Lieut MACFARLANE & party i/c R.E. Store Dumps in RUMAUCOURT. Q.25.&26. Capt Bourne i/c Transport containing R.E. Stores to be brought forward. Lieut L.J. Giles & Section constructs bridge for wheeled traffic & Field Guns at approx W.9.a.8.8. - Lieut MACSWINEY & Section throw medium Pontoon Bridge across CANAL-DU-NORD at approx Q.34.d.1.8. - II Lieut K Palmer on water reconnaissance. - 3 O.Rs. battle casualties - 1 O.R. 14 days leave to U.K. - Div: Engineer's Bridging Park formed at V.6.a.7.2. - Lieut Kidman takes charge of Horse Lines	W.A.R.B.
BARALLE. W.8.c.2.1.	28th		Company resting with exception of Bridge Maintenance Party - Lieut Macfarlane. leave to U.K. - Sapper GEE transferred to 421st Fd. Coy	W.A.R.B.
	29th		Company moves to RUMACOURT - Lieut Giles takes over Water Supply reconnaissance work from 416th Fd. Coy. - Horse Lines move to P.32.d.4.5. 3 O.Rs rejoin from Hospital - 3 O.Rs. leave to U.K. - Major Murray RAMC attached for water duties	W.A.R.B.
RUMACOURT Q.20.c.7.2.	30th		Bridge at W.9.a.8.8. reconstructed & straightened - Water Supply reconnaissance of OISY-LE-VERGER continued with. - Officer reconnaissances of locks & canals at PALLUEL, bridges over Canal - water levels in CANAL-DU-NORD. - 1 O.R. rejoins from Lewis Gun Course.	W.A.R.B.

W.A.R. Bourne. Captain, R.E.
for O.C. 513 Field Co.

(A7092). Wt. W12839/M1293. 75,0.0. 1/17. D. D. & L., Ltd. Forms/C.2118/14.

51^B S.E.

Instructions regarding War Diaries and Intelligence Summaries are contained in F. S. Regs., Part II. and the Staff Manual respectively. Title pages will be prepared in manuscript.

513TH (LON[illegible]) FIELD COY., R.E.
No. ...... Date ......

WAR DIARY
~~or~~
~~INTELLIGENCE SUMMARY.~~
(Erase heading not required.)

C.R.E. 50[illegible] DIVISION. No. Date 6-11-18

Army Form C. 2118.

Vol 32

Place	Date	Hour	Summary of Events and Information	Remarks and references to Appendices
RUMAUCOURT Q.20.c.7.2.	OCTOBER 1918 1st		No. 4 Sections leaves Coy H.Q. to work on Water Supply in area of VILLERS-LEZ-CAGNICOURT under Lieut Kidman O/c Horse Lines at P.32.d.3.7. where No. 4 Section is accomodated. II Lieut Palmer reconnoitering Locks, Sluices etc & CANALS in PALLEUL - Lieut Giles No. 3 Section on Forward Water Reconnaissance marking of pumps & wells etc. as water tested by Major MURRAY R.A.M.C. - Lieut MacSwiney No. 1 Section principally employed on bridge maintenance. - Medium Pontoon bridges thrown across AGACHE River & CANAL-DU-NORD at Q.23.a.7.7. by OC with assistance of Sappers from 416 & 512 Fld. Coys - bridge (medium pontoon) at Q.34.d.05.70 dismantled. 2 ORs to Hospital. - Water levels at different points taken.	W.A.R.B.
	2nd		Company employed as yesterday chiefly - foot-bridge across CANAL-DU-NORD at Q.17.a.90.20. repaired night 2nd/3rd. 1 OR rejoins from Hospital - 1 OR to Hospital. II LT E J GILES awarded M.C.	W.A.R.B.
	3rd		Work as yesterday - Water Supply - Bridge Maintenance & Repair continued with - Major Murray R.A.M.C. 4 ORs return to unit - 1 OR from leave to U.K. - 1 OR to Officer Cadet Course - England.	W.A.R.B.
	4th		Work as yesterday continued with - Theatre for Divisional Concert Party started.	W.A.R.B.
	5th		No. 1 Section on Bridge maintenance & repair water levels - this work handed over to LIEUT. FARFAN. R.E. 512th Fld Coy R.E. - No. 2 Section on RUMACOURT BATHS (repair) & preparation for installation of Dam at PALLEUL - No. 3 Section on Theatre at VILLERS-LEZ-CAGNICOURT. - No. 4 Section on Baths at V-LEZ-CAGNICOURT. - Lieut MacSWINEY leave to U.K. embarking 6th inst. II LIEUT. E. J. GILES. R.E. awarded Military Cross, 1st Army R. Order 3063 dated [illegible] inst. night 5th/6th Accident at Pontoon Bridge Q.28.d.7.2. - two horses drowned.	W.A.R.B.
	6th		Work as yesterday - No. 2 Section place framework for forming dam in Canal Q.11.a.9.8. - No. 1 Section assist No. 3 Section on Divisional Theatre. - 4 OR leave to U.K.	W.A.R.B.
	7th		Work as yesterday - No. 2 Section dismantle Pontoon Bridge at Q.23.a.7.7. & distribute equipment to 3 Field Coys as ordered by CRE - work carried out at 169th Infy Bde H.Q. - 3 ORs leave to U.K.	W.A.R.B.
	8th		Work continued as yesterday - Capt Bowne with C.Q.M.S.s of 3 Field Coys investigates apparent losses of Pontoon Equipment, everything satisfactrily accounted for. - 3 ORs leave to U.K.	W.A.R.B.
	9th		Work continued - orders received from CRE to make preparations for erection of Lorry Bridge at Q.11.a.9.8. - material for latter collected at night - Trestle Bridge at W.10.a.3.7. dismantled & material collected - 1 OR to hospital - 2 ORs from hospital - 1 OR from R.E. School [illegible]	W.A.R.B.

(A7092). Wt W12839/M1293 75,000 1/17. D. D. & L., Ltd. Forms/C.2118/14.

51.B S.E.

Instructions regarding War Diaries and Intelligence Summaries are contained in F. S. Regs., Part II. and the Staff Manual respectively. Title pages will be prepared in manuscript.

513TH (LONDON) FIELD COY. R.E.

No .... Date ....

WAR DIARY
or
~~INTELLIGENCE SUMMARY.~~
(Erase heading not required.)

Army Form C. 2118.

Place	Date OCTOBER.	Hour	Summary of Events and Information	Remarks and references to Appendices
RUMACOURT Q.20.c.7.2.	10th		No. 1 Section - repair of foot bridges over CANAL-DU-NORD - accomodation for 169th Infy. Bde. - No. 2 Section taking trestles & all material forward at night for proposed type "A" bridge at Q.11.a.9.8. - No. 3 Section making trestles & preparing material for latter bridge - No. 4 Section billeted at Horse lines & working on water supply & Bath House VILLERS-LEZ-CAGNICOURT. CRE visits Coy H.Q. & gives orders for a pon bridge to take back axle load of 17 Tons. - 1 OR leave to U.K.	W.A.R.B.
	11th		No. 1 Section as yesterday - No. 2 Section resting - No. 3 Section work on theatre - No. 4 Section as yesterday - 6 ORs reinforcements report from R.E. Base Depot. - Lieut Mefill returns from leave.	W.A.R.B.
	12th		Company employed on erection of Infy foot bridges followed by bridges for Field Guns at Q.11.a.9.8 & Q.5.c.9.7. (Lieut K PALMER & No. 2 Section) - also footbridges over CANAL-DU-NORD - Infy footbridge at Q.35.d.2.2. these works carried out in daylight & dark - Track Q.5.b.0.1 to Q.6.a.20.05 reconnoitred for traffic also main streets through ARLEUX - exceptionally dark night making work difficult (12th-13th) - 1 OR Special leave to U.K. - Lieut Mefill employed on R.A.R.E. under CRE.	W.A.R.B.
	13th		No. 1 Section prepare for erect bridge for Field Guns at Q.35.d.2.2. - No. 4 Section rejoin Company H.Q. in RUMACOURT - Nos. 2 & 3 Sections resting & supplying bridge maintenance party details. bridging Park formed under CAPT. B...	W.A.R.B.
	14th		No. 4 Composite Section stand by with Pontoons in ECOURT-ST QUENTIN at dawn for throwing Pontoon Bridge across SENSEE CANAL at K.36.b.8.2. in event of Infy. advance - all bridges in PALLUEL & ARLEUX - braced & strengthened.	W.A.R.B.
	15th		Company relieved by 11 Bat. Canadian Engineers - Transport moves to MAROEUIL by road during day - ... return to Company - Sappers erect dam at Q.11.a.9.8. dismantling same later in day - Sappers under OC entrain at MARQUION for MAROEUIL 0030 % night 15th-16th - Lieut Macfarlane returns from leave to U.K.	W.A.R.B.
MAROEUIL	16th		Company resting after arriving in new billets - 1 OR to hospital - 1 OR from leave to U.K.	W.A.R.B.
	17th		Company employed on interior economy work - Pontoons, trestles & all Bridging Equipment handed over to Canadian Corps as per instructions of CRE. - 4 ORs from leave.	W.A.R.B.
	18th		As yesterday - 2 ORs to Hospital - 3 ORs from R.E. Base Depot - 1 OR from Hospital - 6 ORs leave to U.K.	W.A.R.B.
	19th		Two hours training - clipping of Horses commenced - 4 ORs leave to U.K. - LIEUT GILES leaves for 14 days leave U.K.	W.A.R.B.

(A7092). Wt. W12839/M1293. 750,000. 1/17. D. D. & L., Ltd. Forms/C.2118/14.

Instructions regarding War Diaries and Intelligence Summaries are contained in F. S. Regs., Part II. and the Staff Manual respectively. Title pages will be prepared in manuscript.

513TH (LONDON) FIELD COY., R.E.
No..........
Date..........

WAR DIARY
or
~~INTELLIGENCE SUMMARY.~~
(*Erase heading not required.*)

Army Form C. 2118.

Place	Date	Hour	Summary of Events and Information	Remarks and references to Appendices
MAROEUIL	20.		Church Parade	ADS
	21.		Company training for 5 hours 1 O.R. leave to U.K. 1 O.R. joined from Base. LIEUT F.E. MACSWINEY rejoined unit from leave.	ADS
	22.		5 hours co: training 4 O.R's leave to U.K. 1 OR from hospital 4 OR ~~from~~ to leave.	ADS
	23.		5 hours Coy Training. 3 OR leave to UK. 1 OR to Base Depot.	ADS
	24.		5 hours Coy Training 5 OR leave to UK 4 OR rejoined from leave	ADS
	25.		5 hours Coy Training 7 OR leave to UK 4 OR " from leave.	ADS
	26		5 hours Coy Training. II LIEUT A.H. NAYLOR joined from Base	ADS
	27.		2 OR rejoined from leave. Church Parade. LIEUT [illegible]	ADS
	28.		Berthon Boat Practise at ARRAS. II LIEUT A H NAYLOR [illegible] LIEUT M MACFARLANE 4 days leave to PARIS 1 OR leave to UK.	ADS
	29		Instruction to 167 Inf Bde Infantry in Berthon Boats at [illegible] 1 OR leave to U.K.	ADS
	30.		" to 168 " " " " " " at [illegible] W.A.R. BOURNE to hospital. 2 OR to hospital	ADS
	31.		Dismounted portion of Company moves to PAVE DE VALENCIENNES by [illegible] mounted portion by road to MARQUION	ADS

A D S[illegible]
Major R.E.(T)
513th (London) Field Coy R.E.

(A7092). Wt W12839/M1293. 75,0.0. 1/17. D. D. & L., Ltd. Forms/C.2118/14.

Army Form C. 2118.

WAR DIARY
or
~~INTELLIGENCE SUMMARY.~~
(Erase heading not required.)

Instructions regarding War Diaries and Intelligence Summaries are contained in F. S. Regs., Part II. and the Staff Manual respectively. Title pages will be prepared in manuscript.

C.R.E. ~~56th~~ DIVISION No. 3.12.18.

513TH (LONDON) FIELD COY., R.E.

VR 33

Place	Date 1918.	Hour	Summary of Events and Information	Remarks and references to Appendices
PAVÉ	Nov. 1st.		Mounted portion of company rejoins from MARQUION. 1 trestle wagon + 2 pontoons taken over from Corps and the 3 empty trestle wagons handed over to Corps.	[initials]
ditto.	2ND.		Company moves to THIANT. 11.45 hrs. Guard of 2 men placed on Bridge at MAING. 1 cycle was lost during trek. ~~1 OR. from leave to U.K.~~	[initials]
THIANT.	3RD.		No 4 section employed on clearing debris at Bridge at MAING. Lieut goes on reconnaissance of Road Craters at SAULTAIN. Lieut Kidman goes on reconnaissance for R.E. Stores. II Lt Palmer visits Bde re. forward work. 1 OR. from leave to U.K.	[initials]
ditto.	4th.		Company moves to ~~SEBOURG A20d09~~ SAULTAIN at 1100. LT Kidman + M. Carrie go on reconnaissance of RE Stores. II Lt Palmer with No 2 Section joins Bde for work in forward area. Lt Machvinny in charge of Transport. II Lt Palmer + No 2 Section still with Bde	[initials]
SAULTAIN	5th.		Company moves to SEBOURG A20d09. 2 OR. attached to 86 M.I. Coy.	[initials]
SEBOURG SHEET 51. A20d.09.	6th.		Company employed on heavy Bridge under 512 Field Coy. Capt W.A.B. Bourne rejoins from Hospital and leave to take over command of 84 F. Coy R.E. II Lt Giles from leave to U.K. 1 OR. from leave to U.K.	[initials]
ditto.	7th.		1 3 + 4 Section employed with 512 Field Company constructing heavy bridge at A14.c.8.6. No 2. Section employed with Bde in the line. Company move to ANGREAU A17b.30. at 1500 hrs. 6 OR from leave to U.K. 2 OR from Hospl. 2 OR. rejoin from M.O. Lt Macfarlane from leave in France. Lt McSwinney + 1 OR. attached 416 F. Coy. RE.	[initials]

(A7092). Wt. W12839/M1293. 751,000. 1/17. D. D. & L., Ltd. Forms/C.2118/14.

Instructions regarding War Diaries and Intelligence Summaries are contained in F. S. Regs., Part II. and the Staff Manual respectively. Title pages will be prepared in manuscript.

WAR DIARY
or
~~INTELLIGENCE SUMMARY.~~
(Erase heading not required.)

510TH (LONDON) FIELD COY. R.E.

Army Form C. 2118.

Place	Date	Hour	Summary of Events and Information	Remarks and references to Appendices
AUTREPPE B19 c 77. SHEET 51.	1918. Nov. 8th		1. 3 + 4. Sections employed on moving obstacles + building trestle bridge. at B2 c 20 ~~II Lt Palmer + No 2 Section are relieved by 512 Field Coy at 1100.~~	[initials]
ditto.	9th		Company working on Roads. 1 O.R. to Hosp. 8 O.R. from Hospl. II Lt Palmer + No 2 Section are relieved by 512 F Coy. RE. 1 O.R. to Hospl.	[initials]
ditto.	10th		Work on Roads continues. Company moves to FAYT LEFRANC ~~B19~~ B18 a 5.4. at 1130. No 2 Section building bridge for lorries. II Lt Gill rejoins company from C.R.E. 4 O.R. rejoin from leave to U.K.	[initials]
FAYT LEFRANC B19 a 5.4.	11th		Work on Roads continues. News received that Armistice is sign, Hostilities cease at 1100 hrs. 4 O.R. rejoin from leave to U.K. 2 O.R. reinforcements join Coy.	[initials]
ditto	12th.		Work on Roads continues, general cleaning up of vehicles + Harness. 4 O.R. to leave to U.K. 15-29. 12 O.R. rejoin from leave to U.K.	[initials]
ditto	13th.		One Section only employed on Roads. Remainder working in camp + cleaning up. 2 O.R. from Hospl.	[initials]
ditto	14th		One Section continues work on Roads. Remainder working on cleaning vehicles + equipment	[initials]
ditto.	15th.		Work as yesterday. 5 O.R. making tables for office + mess. ~~Lt MacSwiney + 1 O.R. rejoin from 416 Field Coy. R.E. 1 O.R. from Base 3 O.R. from leave to UK~~	[initials]
ditto.	16th.		One Section working on Roads. 4 O.R. making forms for church Service. Remainder cleaning up equipment + vehicles.	[initials]

(A7092). Wt. W12839/M1293. 750,000. 1/17. D. D. & L., Ltd. Forms/C.2118/14.

Instructions regarding War Diaries and Intelligence Summaries are contained in F. S. Regs., Part II. and the Staff Manual respectively. Title pages will be prepared in manuscript.

WAR DIARY

~~or~~

~~INTELLIGENCE SUMMARY.~~

(Erase heading not required.)

513TH (LONDON) FIELD COY., R.E.

No. ....

Date ....

Army Form C. 2118.

Place	Date 1918	Hour	Summary of Events and Information	Remarks and references to Appendices
FAYT LE FRANC SHEET 51. B18a.5.4.	Nov. 17.		One Section employed on Road repair + maintenance. Two Sections building heavy Bridge at V.22b.2.6. Major Steers + Lt McGill reconnoitred ~~this~~ early this morning. One Section working on companies vehicles + equipment. 7 O.R rejoin from leave to U.K. 1 O.R. to Hospl.	MHR
	18th		One Section continues on Road work. Remainder of Company Resting. 3 O.R. employed as Bridge at V22b2.6 maintenance party. 1 O.R. to U.K on leave.	MHR
	19th		One Section continues on Road repairs. Remainder on making seats + tables etc for Bdes + Recreation Rooms. Major Steers acting CRE while CRE is on leave. 1 O.R. to Hospl. 2 O.R. rejoin from leave to U.K.	MHR
	20th		Work as yesterday. 1 O.R to Hospl.	MHR
	21th		One Section on Road work. Remainder preparing recreation rooms + seating for Bow Bells + Cinema. Special church at 1100 in School Room. 1 O.R from Hospl. 6 O.R. rejoin from leave to U.K. 1 O.R to leave to U.K.	MHR
	22nd		One Section continues on Road work. Remainder on Horses cleaning + general Company work. 2nd Lieut L.D. Stamp RE reports for duty from Base. Lt McGill ~~takes~~ acting Adjutant to CRE. 14 O.R rejoin from leave to U.K.	MHR
	23rd		Two Sections employed on making Seating for Cinema + Bow Bells. Remainder of company cleaning up for inspection + improving billets. 2 O.R to Hospital.	MHR

Instructions regarding War Diaries and Intelligence Summaries are contained in F. S. Regs., Part II. and the Staff Manual respectively. Title pages will be prepared in manuscript.

WAR DIARY
or
~~INTELLIGENCE SUMMARY.~~
(Erase heading not required.)

513TH (LONDON) FIELD COY., R.E.
No ....
Date ....

Army Form C. 2118.

Place	Date	Hour	Summary of Events and Information	Remarks and references to Appendices
FAYT LE FRANC SHEET 51 B18a.5.4.	1918 Nov. ~~24th~~		~~Two Sections finishing + fixing Seats + Cinema Box. Remainder preparing to move~~ ~~3 O.R. from leave to UK 1 O.R. to Hospl.~~	MM
	~~25th~~ 24th		Rest Day. 3 O.R. rejoin from leave to UK 1 O.R. to Hospl.	MM
	25th		Two Sections finishing + fixing Seats + Box in Cinema. Remainder of Company preparing to move. 1 O.R. rejoins from leave to U.K.	MM
	26th		Company moves under the Command of Capt. M. Macfarlane at 0920 hrs to join Bde Column at 1013. Arrive BOUGNIES. (SHEET 45. W 19a. at 1645 hrs.	MM
BOUGNIES SHEET 45. W.19a.1.5.	27th		Settling in Billets + adjusting where necessary. Making latrines etc. II Lt Palmer continues with educational organization.	MM
	28th		Company parade at 0900 hrs. Rifle + equipment inspection. Cleaning vehicles, etc. 4 O.R. to leave to U.K.	MM
	29th		Company moves to ASQUILLIES at 1130 hrs. Arrive 1230. Horses + Drivers return to billets at BOUGNIES as there is not accommodation for them at ASQUILLIES. Lt Crossfield + 2 O.R. attached for rations. 2 O.R. to leave U.K. 1 O.R. to Hospl.	MM
ASQUILLIES SHEET 45 W.8.c.8.8.	30		Section employed on making latrines etc. No 4. Section under Lt Kidman go to NOUVELLES to get two A.S.C. wagons out of river. 1 O.R. to leave U.K.	MM

M Macfarlane Capt R.E.(T)
for OC 513th (London) Field Coy R.E.

(A7092). Wt W12839/M1293. 75,0.0. 1/17. D. D. & L., Ltd. Forms/C.2118/14.

Instructions regarding War Diaries and Intelligence Summaries are contained in F. S. Regs., Part II. and the Staff Manual respectively. Title pages will be prepared in manuscript.

WAR DIARY
or
~~INTELLIGENCE~~ SUMMARY.

(Erase heading not required.)

Army Form C. 2118.

513 London Field Coy. R.E.

No. 513 4th Coy RE 98 34

Place	Date 1918	Hour	Summary of Events and Information	Remarks and references to Appendices
ASQUILLIES SHEET 45	DEC. 1		Company employed on cleaning up roads & billets & preparing to move into finale billets. 1 O.R. to leave to U.K. 1 O.R. from leave to U.K. 1 O.R. from Hosp.	[initials]
~~B.G.~~ W. 8.c.8.8	2.		Company cleaning up village, fixing baths & selecting billets, 4th Div Artillery are moving out tomorrow. 2 O.R. rejoin from leave to U.K.	[initials]
	3.		Move into new billets. Lt MacSwiney with mounted section & all horses move to ASQUILLIES from BOUGNIES at 0900 hrs.	[initials]
	4.		Company employed on washing & parking vehicles, cleaning roads in village, fixing Baths at HARMENIES.	[initials]
	5.		Company less 50 O.R. continue with work as yesterday. Major Steers & Lt Kidman & II Lt Palmer to go for reception of the King at X roads W.14.d.8.6. Whole company bath at 2 – 4 pm.	[initials]
	6.		Company employed on Bde. accommodation, latrines, cookhouse tables & forms etc. II Lt L.D. Stamp & 6 O.R. go on detachment to collect unused bath sets from back areas. Transport employed on drawing material etc. 1 O.R. from leave.	[initials]
	7.		Company employed on Bde accommodation & road repairing. Transport drawing material from MONS. 1 O.R. attached 169 Bde.	[initials]
	8.		Rest day. Transport drawing material as yesterday. 1 O.R. to Hospl. 2 O.R. to leave to U.K. 1 O.R. from 1st Army School of Eng. 1 O.R. from leave. 2 O.R. to 56th M.T. Coy.	[initials]
	9.		Work on Bde accommodation continued. One section on Road cleaning & repair. 1 O.R. from 56th M.T. Coy. 1 O.R. to leave to U.K.	[initials]

Instructions regarding War Diaries and Intelligence Summaries are contained in F. S. Regs., Part II. and the Staff Manual respectively. Title pages will be prepared in manuscript.

WAR DIARY
or
~~INTELLIGENCE~~ SUMMARY.
(Erase heading not required.)

Army Form C. 2118.

Place	Date	Hour	Summary of Events and Information	Remarks and references to Appendices
ASQUILLIES SHEET 45. W.8c.8.8	1918 DEC. 10.		Company employed on Bde accommodation. Road work + cleaning. 3 O.R to leave to U.K. 14 days. 1 O.R. to Corps. Officers Club. ~~1 O.R (miner) to U.K.~~	[illegible]
	11		Work as yesterday. 1 O.R. (miner) to U.K. 1 O.R. leave to U.K.	[illegible]
	12.		Work on Bde accommodation continues. Also making tables + forms etc for educational purposes. 1 O.R. to leave to U.K. 3 officers + 84 O.R. of 179 Tunnelling Coy attached for Rations. 1 O.R. to Hospl.	[illegible]
	13.		Work as yesterday. 2 O.R. to U.K. (miners) 38 O.Rs from Bde attached for instruction 2 O.R. to leave to U.K. 1 O.R. from Hospl. 2 O.R. from leave to U.K.	[illegible]
	14.		Work as yesterday continued. Lt W.J. McGill rejoins from C.R.E.'s office. 2 O.R. from leave to U.K.	[illegible]
	15.		Rest day. Church service at 0900 hrs. 2 O.R. rejoin from leave to U.K.	[illegible]
	16.		Work on Bde accommodation, Concert Hall ~~etc~~ Roads etc continues. 2 O.R. rejoin from leave to U.K. 2 O.R. to leave to U.K.	[illegible]
	17.		Work on Bde accommodation Roads etc continues. 1 O.R. rejoins from leave to U.K. 1 O.R. to leave to U.K.	[illegible]
	18.		Work as yesterday. 53 OR + 7 officers to Bde H.Q. at 1700 to see "Bow Bells". 1 O.R. rejoins from leave. 1 O.R. to leave U.K.	[illegible]

D. D. & L., London, E.C.
(10340) W: W5300/P713 750,000 3/18 E 2688 Forms/C2118/16.

Instructions regarding War Diaries and Intelligence Summaries are contained in F. S. Regs., Part II. and the Staff Manual respectively. Title pages will be prepared in manuscript.

WAR DIARY
or
~~INTELLIGENCE SUMMARY.~~
(Erase heading not required.)

513TH (LONDON) FIELD COY., R.E.
No.........
Date.........

Army Form C. 2118.

Place	Date 1918.	Hour	Summary of Events and Information	Remarks and references to Appendices
ASQUILLIES. SHEET 45 W8c88.	DEC 19.		Company employed on Brigade accommodation. Repairs to Roads & Building Bridges at ASQUILLIES W8d0595 and at NOUVELLES W3a97. 2 O.R. to leave to U.K.	[initials]
	20.		Work as yesterday. 1 O.R. to leave to U.K.	[initials]
	21.		Company employed as yesterday. Bridge at ASQUILLIES completed. 1 O.R. to leave to U.K.	[initials]
	22.		Work as yesterday, one section employed on clearing site of masonry bridge at ASQUILLIES. 1 O.R. to leave to U.K. 2 O.R. rejoin from leave to U.K.	[initials]
	23.		Work continues as yesterday. CRE returns from leave. Major Steers rejoins from CRE's Office. 1 O.R. to leave to U.K. 1 O.R. rejoins from leave to U.K.	[initials]
	24.		Work as yesterday. Attached men return to their units for Xmas. 1 O.R. to leave to U.K. 1 O.R. rejoins from leave to U.K.	[initials]
	25.		Observed as a Rest day. Church Parade at 1130 hrs. Church Service in the School room. 2 O.R. 14 days leave to U.K.	[initials]
	26.		Work on Bde accommodation, shelters etc resumed. Attached men for instruction do not return today. 1 O.R. 14 days leave to U.K. 1 O.R. rejoins from leave	[initials]
	27.		Work continued as yesterday. Lt McGill & II Lt Stamps make a survey of inundation at NOUVELLES. 1 O.R. to U.K. demobilised long service.	[initials]

D. D. & L., London, E.C.
(10349) W1 W5300/P713 750,000 3/18 E 2688 Forms/C/2118/16.

Instructions regarding War Diaries and Intelligence Summaries are contained in F. S. Regs., Part II. and the Staff Manual respectively. Title pages will be prepared in manuscript.

WAR DIARY
or
~~INTELLIGENCE SUMMARY.~~
(Erase heading not required.)

513TH (LONDON) FIELD COY., R.E.
No. ...
Date ...

Army Form C. 2118.

Place	Date 1918	Hour	Summary of Events and Information	Remarks and references to Appendices
ASQUILLIES	DEC. 28th		Company employed on Bde accommodation, Erecting Sheds, Rebuilding Brick Bridge making Stoves, etc. 1 OR 14 days leave to U.K.	M.M.
SHEET 45	29.		Rest day. Inspection of Boots + equipment. OC reads out Demobilization Wire.	M.M.
W.8.c.8.8.	30.		Work continues as on Monday. 3OR under Lt Stamp removing Road Mine. 25OR are taken by lorry to Mons at 1800 hrs to see Bow Bells.	M.M.
	31.		Work as yesterday. 1OR. 14 days leave to U.K.	M.M.

M. Macfarlane
Captain, R.E.
for O.C. 513 Field Co.

513TH (LONDON) FIELD COY., R.E.
No. ...
Date 4/1/1919

D. D. & L., London, E.C.
(10340) Wt W5300/P713 750,000 3/18 E 2688 Forms/C/2118/15.

Instructions regarding War Diaries and Intelligence Summaries are contained in F. S. Regs., Part II. and the Staff Manual respectively. Title pages will be prepared in manuscript.

WAR DIARY
or
~~INTELLIGENCE SUMMARY.~~
(Erase heading not required.)

513

Army Form C. 2118.

Place	Date	Hour	Summary of Events and Information	Remarks and references to Appendices
ASQUILLIES SHEET 45. W.8.C.8.8.	1919. JAN. 1.		Company employed on Carpentry work for Bde. Repairs to Road. Rebuilding Brick Bridge. also building temporary Bridge. at Sheet 51. D.5.b.5.6.. 4 O.R. reinforcements join for duty from Base. 1 O.R. rejoins from leave.	[signature]
	2.		Work continues as yesterday. 2 O.R. 14 days leave to UK. 3 O.R. rejoin from leave	[signature]
	3.		Work as yesterday ~~5~~ 4 O.R. rejoin from leave. 1 O.R. rejoins from Hospt. 1 O.R. awarded 10 days C.B. ~~[illegible]~~ 1 O.R. to UK as WATFORD DETAIL. IILt K. Palmer to Hospital.	[signature]
	4.		Work continues as yesterday. IILt Stamp + Sergt Bush to SOIGNIES for Stone for rebuilding Bridge at ASQUILLIES. Lt Kidman to UK as conducting officer. 1 O.R. from leave.	[signature] [signature]
	5.		Rest Day.	
	6.		Work on Bde accommodation, building Brick Bridge at ASQUILLIES. Wagon repairs + painting etc. continued. 1 O.R. rejoins from leave	[signature]
	7.		Work as yesterday. 3 O.R. rejoin from leave to UK	[signature]
	8.		Work continues as yesterday.	[signature]
	9.		Work as yesterday. Company Play Div. League match against 2nd London Regt.	[signature]

D. D. & L., London, E.C. (10340) Wt W5300/P713 750,000 3/18 E 2688 Forms C/2118/16.

Army Form C. 2118.

Instructions regarding War Diaries and Intelligence Summaries are contained in F. S. Regs., Part II. and the Staff Manual respectively. Title pages will be prepared in manuscript.

WAR DIARY
or
~~INTELLIGENCE~~ SUMMARY.

(Erase heading not required.)

513th (LONDON) FIELD COY., R.E.

Place	Date	Hour	Summary of Events and Information	Remarks and references to Appendices
ASQUILLIES SHEET 45 W8e88	1919 JAN. 10.		Work on Bde requirements. etc. Bridges + Road repair continues. 6 O.R. to UK for demobilization. CRE addresses	MM.
	11.		Work continues as yesterday. 1 O.R. rejoins from Hospital. 1 O.R. to Hospital. 7. O.R. to U.K. for demobilisation.	MM.
	12.		Rest day. 30 R working on special job ~~[illegible]~~ 1 O.R. rejoins from leave UK. 1 O.R. to UK for demobilisation	MM.
	13.		Work on Bridge at ASQUILLIES continues also Carpenters + Plumbers + Painters on various jobs. 1. OR to UK for demob.	MM.
	14.		Work continues as yesterday. 4 O.R. to UK for demob. 3 O.R. attached for instruction. 1 O.R. rejoins from Hospital. 21 attached men return to their units	MM.
	15.		Work continues as yesterday but work on Bridge materially slowed because of attached men being recalled to their units.	MM.
	16.		Work as yesterday.	MM.
	17.		Work continues as yesterday.	MM.
	18.		Work as yesterday. Bde accommodation. Building Bridge at Asquillies building sheds for D.A.D.O.S. etc. 1 O.R. joins from Base for Orderly Room.	MM.
	19.		Rest day.	MM.
	20.		Work on Bridge. Ration dump, D.A.D.O.S sheds + Carpenters shops continues. 10. O.R. to U.K. for demob. Lt Palmer returns from Hospital	MM.

D. D. & L., London, E.C.
(10340) W: W5300/P713 750,000 3/18 E 2688 Forms C/2118/16.

3

Army Form C. 2118.

WAR DIARY
or
~~INTELLIGENCE SUMMARY.~~

(Erase heading not required.)

Instructions regarding War Diaries and Intelligence Summaries are contained in F. S. Regs., Part II. and the Staff Manual respectively. Title pages will be prepared in manuscript.

Place	Date 1919	Hour	Summary of Events and Information	Remarks and references to Appendices
ASQUILLIES SHEET 45 W8c98	JAN. 21.		Work on Bridge, Ration dump, DADOS Shed & Carpenters shop. Cpt Macfarlane to UK Demob. 14 O.R. to U.K. for Demobilisation. 2 O.R. to Hospital.	F.E.M.
	22		Work on Bridge, Ration Dump, work in Carpenters shop. 5 O.R. to U.K. Demob. 1 OR rejoins from Hosp.	F.E.M.
	23		Work on Bridge, Ration Dump, Bath Set, Carpenters shop.	F.E.M.
	24		Work on Bridge, Ration dump, Cook House D.A.D.O.S. 1 O.R. rejoined from Hosp.	F.E.M.
	25		Work as yesterday. 4 OR to U.K. demob. 1 OR. to U.K. Leave	F.E.M.
	26		Rest day. 10 OR to U.K. Demob. Sergt Miller awarded M.S.M	F.E.M.
	27		Work on Bridge. 7 OR. to U.K. for Demob. 1 OR. rejoins from Leave	F.E.M.
	28		Work as yesterday. 9 O.R. to U.K. for Demob. Lt. McGill to UK Demob.	F.E.M.
	29		Work on Bridge, Disinfestator for Brigade, Hut for D.A.D.O.S., work in Carpenters shop. 10 O.R. to U.K. for Demobilisation	F.E.M.
	30		Work on Disinfestator. Hut for D.A.D.O.S. Erecting Bath set. 1 OR. returned from hospital	F.E.M.
	31		Work on Disinfestator, Hut for D.A.D.O.S., Bath set, Hut for Coy. 1 OR att. returns to his unit	F.E.M.
			F. E. MacSwiney Lt R.E.T. a/OC 513 Field Coy RE	1.2.19.

(A7092). Wt. W12839/M1293. 75,0 0. 1/17. D. D. & L., Ltd. Forms/C.2118/14.

Instructions regarding War Diaries and Intelligence Summaries are contained in F. S. Regs., Part II. and the Staff Manual respectively. Title pages will be prepared in manuscript.

WAR DIARY

~~or~~

~~INTELLIGENCE SUMMARY.~~

(Erase heading not required.)

513 Fd Coy RE

Army Form C. 2118.

Vol 36

Place	Date	Hour	Summary of Events and Information	Remarks and references to Appendices
	1919 FEB			
ASQUILLIES	1.		WORK – Erecting Shed for D.A.D.O.S – Erecting Nissen Hut for Coy: – Erecting Bath House for Coy: –	
Map Ref:			Making Disinfestator – Erecting stoves for 2nd LON: O.C. to U.K: 14 d-leave. 11 O.R. U.K. Demob:	R.H.
BELGIUM AND PART OF FRANCE	2.		SUNDAY – Company resting – 2 Lt L.D. STAMP. att: R.E.H.Q as Demob: officer. 7 O.R. to U.K. Demob:	R.H.
SHEET 45 Ed. 3	3.		WORK – Shed for D.A.D.O.S – Nissen Hut for Coy & bath House. ~~11~~ 10. R.H. O.R. to U.K. Demob: 9/ckk(?) & 4/ckk Kinnear(?) Sgt Brown A.B. app.d 12/1/19	R.H.
1:40.000.	4.		WORK – Shed for D.A.D.O.S – Bath House for Coy. 140775 Sapper Morris W. raised to Skilled Rate P.P. 1/11/18	R.H.
W.8.C.88.	5.		WORK – As yesterday –	R.H.
	6.		WORK – Erecting Disinfestator – HARMIGNIES. Erecting NISSENS for 282 R.F.A. 1 O.R. to U.K for Demob	R.H.
	7.		WORK – Roping in Footer ground for Div. Cup tie. HARMIGNIES. – NISSENS for 282 R.F.A. Disinfestator erecting, HARMIGNIES – 2 O.R. to U.K. Demob:	R.H.
	8.		WORK – Dismantling Concert Hall, HARMIGNIES – NISSEN HUTS for 282 R.F.A. – Repairs to Bridge NOUVILLES, W3097 – Fitting stoves for D.A.D.O.S.	R.H.
	9.		SUNDAY. Company resting – less small party working on Bridge at NOUVILLES. 1 O.R. to U.K. Demob: 1 O.R. att. for Eds Training rejoins Unit.	R.H.
	10.		WORK – Disinfestator erecting, HARMIGNIES – NISSEN HUTS for 282 R.F.A. Repairing railings at D.H.Q. 1 O.R. rejoins from leave to U.K. –	R.H.
	11.		WORK – Fitting up lighting set at L.R.B. Chateau – HARMIGNIES – Repairing railing at D.H.Q. Erecting NISSEN Huts for 282 R.F.A.	R.H.

(A9175) Wt W2353/P363 600,000 12/17 D. D. & L. Sch. 52a. Forms/C2118/15.

Instructions regarding War Diaries and Intelligence Summaries are contained in F. S. Regs., Part II, and the Staff Manual respectively. Title pages will be prepared in manuscript.

WAR DIARY
~~or~~
~~INTELLIGENCE SUMMARY.~~
(Erase heading not required.)

Army Form C. 2118.

Place	1919 Date	Hour	Summary of Events and Information	Remarks and references to Appendices
ASQUILLIES (SHEET 45.) W8C88	12th Feb.		WORK – Fitting Electric light set L.R.B. CHATEAU HARMIGNIES. Erecting NISSEN Huts for 282 RFA.	F.B.h.
	13		WORK – Light set HARMIGNIES. NISSEN Huts for 282 RFA. Repairing handrail ASQUILLIES Bridge. 1 OR UK 14 days leave	F.B.h.
	14		WORK – Light set HARMIGNIES. Making latrines for Dados.	F.B.h.
	15		WORK – 5 OR. detailed to work for 512 RE at QUEVY-le-GRAND. Lighting set HARMIGNIES. Latrine for D.A.D.O.S. Spr Fellows struck off strength Demob, while on leave. 4 OR. att to Coy for Educational training returned to their Units. Major Stern rejoins from leave to UK. 1 OR leave to UK – 1 OR. Rejoins from leave to UK.	F.B.h.
	16.		WORK. 6 OR work for 512 RE – Lighting Set. 8 OR. observe Rest day.	F.B.h.
	17.		WORK. 3 OR work for 513 RE – Lighting set. 6 OR observe Rest day. 1 OR. rejoins from leave to U.K. 1 L.D. Transfer M.V.S (for Sale)	F.B.h.
	18		WORK. Lighting set – Preparing Football for Div [illegible] – Final. 1 OR to UK leave	F.B.h.
	19		WORK. Lighting Set. Dismantling baths HARVENGT. 1 OR to UK leave. 18 Animals to No 4 Base. 5 OR on convoy	F.B.h.
	20		WORK. Lighting set – Bath set – Re-roping Football field. Cpl Macleod apt A/Sgt Pd 20/1/19. Cpl Lill apt A/Sgt Pd 21/1/19. L/Cpl Adam apt A/Cpl Pd 20/1/19. L/Cpl Bittrell apt A/Cpl Pd 21/1/19. Spr Hamilton apt A/2nd Cpl Pd 20/1/19. 2nd Cpl Palmer apt A/Cpl Pd 6/2/19. Spr Barnes apt A/L/Cpl Pd 21/1/19. Spr Kempster apt A/2nd Cpl Pd 21/1/19. Spr Humiston apt A/L/Cpl Pd 21/1/19. L/Cpl Patten apt A/Cpl Pd 6/2/19.	F.B.h.

Instructions regarding War Diaries and Intelligence Summaries are contained in F. S. Regs., Part II. and the Staff Manual respectively. Title pages will be prepared in manuscript.

WAR DIARY
or
INTELLIGENCE SUMMARY.
(Erase heading not required.)

Army Form C. 2118.

Place	Date	Hour	Summary of Events and Information	Remarks and references to Appendices
ASQUILLIES	1919 Feb.			
SHEET 45.	21		WORK. Making latrines for D.A.D.O.S. – Bath set repairs ASQUILLIES – 2 OR to UK leave	H.D.S.
W8.C.88	23		SUNDAY – Rest day. 1 OR. leave to U.K. 2 LD to M.V.S.	H.D.S.
	22		Repairs to Bath sets. Dismantling football field HARMIGNIES	H.D.S.
	24		Erecting Bath set VILLERS-SIRE-NICOLE. Ect Disinfestator. Return tools used for Refresher courses to Corps Dump. Major Steers attends Army Conference. 1st Lt Wilkins struck off strength as from 8/1/19. ~~[illegible]~~	H.D.S.
	25		Erecting Bath at VILLERS-SIRE-NICOLE. Disinfestator, Arranging Football Ground Div final. 4 LD, 1 R = 5 animals to No. 4 Base, 1 OR at cond. party. 4 Animals to M.V.S, 1 OR cond. party.	H.D.S.
	26		Corps Race Meeting 2 Off & 19 OR attend. 1 OR. leave to UK, Cpl Brearley awarded M.M.	H.D.S.
	27.		WORK. Moving & collecting Surplus Stores to MONS (ARSENAL DUMP)	H.D.S.
	28.		Checking co. equipt & cleaning same.	H.D.S.

H D Steers

D.C. 613 (LOND) FIELD COY, R.E.

Instructions regarding War Diaries and Intelligence Summaries are contained in F. S. Regs., Part II, and the Staff Manual respectively. Title pages will be prepared in manuscript.

WAR DIARY
or
INTELLIGENCE SUMMARY.
(Erase heading not required.)

513th Field Co RE

Army Form C. 2118.

Vol 37

Place	Date	Hour	Summary of Events and Information	Remarks and references to Appendices
ASQUILLES	1		LD mare Evac to No 4 Base. Work checking & cleaning equip	
Sheet 45	2		Sgt MacSwiney to Hospital. Sr Palmer 14 days leave to UK. Work as above	
W 8 c 8 8	3		a/L/Cpl Patten Dr Scarfe Walker James Moore Rejoin from Horse conducting "	
	4		Cpl McInnes to UK demob. 1 Rider 1 LD (Z) animals to Mob Vet Section	
	5		7 LD 3 riders (Z) animals Sale at Givry. Sgt Bush 14 leave UK.	
	6		Sgt C.C. MacLeod rejoins from French leave	
	7		Dr Smith rejd from Horse conducting. Spr Tyldesley Off strgth 1/3/19	
	8		Spr Cobb 524499 raised to Sup rate from 1/3/19	
	9		3 LD horses evac to No 4 Base Remt Depot. Spr Eastham	
	10		Spr Graham rejoins from UK leave / Spr Stacey Dr Sewer from UK	
	11		3 LD horses & 2 mules to Givry for sale	
	12		Repair bridge ASQUILLES	
	13		Dismantled Officers cook house	
	14		5 LD mules 2 R horses 3 LD horses to Cologne 4 strings	
	15		Spr Moffat A rejoined from leave UK. Spr Macdonald from hand mare	
	16		Spr Messer raised to skilled rate as from 1/2/19	

E J Giles

Instructions regarding War Diaries and Intelligence Summaries are contained in F. S. Regs., Part II. and the Staff Manual respectively. Title pages will be prepared in manuscript.

WAR DIARY
or
INTELLIGENCE SUMMARY.
(Erase heading not required.)

Army Form C. 2118.

Place	Date	Hour	Summary of Events and Information	Remarks and references to Appendices
ASQUILLIES	17		Spr McDonald Dvr Hoffman posted to 1/10 Coy RE [illegible]	
	18		36 mules to Rouen Dvr Scarfe horse conduct to Rouen	
	19		Lt K Palmer rejoins from leave S/S Bircham apt A/L Cpl from 1/1/19	
JEMAPPES	20		Company moves to Jemappes Bath at [illegible]	
	21		Major Steen [illegible] Smith [illegible] from horse conduct Cpl Phelps [illegible]	
	22		Sgt Bush rejoins unit from leave to UK.	
	23		Capt [illegible], 14 days leave to UK. 24.3.19 – 7.4.19	
	24		Dvr Scarfe rejoined unit from horse conducting duty. Evacuated 2 L.D. horses – (X) Checking stores etc as per [illegible] Regs.	
	25		1 L.D. horse from Div[l] Signals brought on strength.	
	26		2 Lt Stamp RE whilst on detachment [illegible] posted to clearing up Army, 1st Base Park Coy & permanently struck of strength of the unit.	
	27		2 L.D. horses evacuated unit to No 4 Remount Depot	
	27		Lt E J Gilbert [illegible] unit this day to 20 Defence [illegible] 1st Army	

K Palmer Lt
513th Field Coy RE

(A9175) Wt W2358/P360 600,000 12/17 D. D. & L. Sch. 52a. Forms/C2118/15.

Army Form C. 2118.

WAR DIARY
or
INTELLIGENCE SUMMARY.
(Erase heading not required.)

Instructions regarding War Diaries and Intelligence Summaries are contained in F. S. Regs., Part II. and the Staff Manual respectively. Title pages will be prepared in manuscript.

Place	Date	Hour	Summary of Events and Information	Remarks and references to Appendices
JEMAPPES	27		Lt. Wood rejoined unit from Base conducting	
			Lt. Nash. struck off strength of unit as from 10.1.19	
			authy RE BR letter of 18/3/19.	
	29		Pte Hatch & Spr Osborne evacuated unit today for	
			transfer to 204 Supply Coy.	
	31		Lt. Dodd. 14 days leave to UK 31/3/19 – 14.4.19.	

Palmer Lt R.E. Capt
5/3rd Field Co RE.

(A9175) Wt W2358/P360 500,000 12/17 D. D. & L. Sch. 52a. Forms/C2118/15.

Instructions regarding War Diaries and Intelligence Summaries are contained in F. S. Regs., Part II. and the Staff Manual respectively. Title pages will be prepared in manuscript.

WAR DIARY
or
~~INTELLIGENCE SUMMARY.~~
(Erase heading not required.)

Army Form C. 2118.

513 Fd Coy RE

Vol 38

Place	Date	Hour	Summary of Events and Information	Remarks and references to Appendices
	APRIL 1919			
JEMEPPES MONS	1		One O.R. to UK 14 days leave.	F.R.h.
	2		NIL.	F.R.h
	3			F.R.h
	4		5 O.R. depart for Army of Occupation, posted to 9th Lowland Div	F.R.h
	5		2 OR. to U.K. 14 days leave 3 OR escort duty from Rouen.	F.R.h
	6		2 OR. to U.K. 14 days leave	F.R.h
	7		NIL.	F.R.h
	8			
	9		Capt. F.R. MacSwiney return from leave U.K. 1 OR to Hospital.	F.R.h
	11		3 OR return from Rouen, escort duty. 1 OR from leave U.K. 1 OR rejoins from Hospital	F.R.h
	12		Lieut K. Palmer & 3 OR attached to D.A.D.E.S MONS.	F.R.h
	13 & 14		NIL.	F.R.h
	15		1 OR to UK leave 14 days.	F.R.h
	16		2 OR to UK leave 14 days.	F.R.h
	17		1 OR to UK, leave 14 days.	F.R.h
	18		2 OR to UK, leave 14 days	F.R.h.

F.R. MacSwiney Captain, R.E.
O.C. 513 Field Co.

(A9175) Wt W2358/P360 600,000 12/17 D. D. & L. Sch. 52a. Forms/C2118/15.

Army Form C. 2118.

Instructions regarding War Diaries and Intelligence Summaries are contained in F. S. Regs., Part II. and the Staff Manual respectively. Title pages will be prepared in manuscript.

WAR DIARY
or
~~INTELLIGENCE SUMMARY.~~
(*Erase heading not required.*)

Place	Date	Hour	Summary of Events and Information	Remarks and references to Appendices
	APRIL 1919			
JEMAPPES MONS.	19. to 21.		NIL.	R.h
	22		1 OR. to UK, 14 days leave	R.h
	23		1 OR from UK, leave. 1 OR. transferred to E.F.C.	R.h
	24		—	R.h
	25		1 OR from UK, leave.	R.h
	26		1 OR to France short leave.	R.h
	27 } 28		NIL	R.h
	29		8 OR motor trip to VALENCIENNES. 2 OR to UK, 14 days leave	R.h
	30.		Lt. K Palmer relieved from DADES. MONS & rejoined unit	R.h

R. Maclaren [?]
Captain, R.E.
O.C. 513 Field Co.

30 APR 1919

(A9175) Wt W2338/P360 600,000 12/17 D. D. & L. Sch. 52a. Forms/C2118/15.

www.ingramcontent.com/pod-product-compliance
Lightning Source LLC
Chambersburg PA
CBHW081410160426
43193CB00013B/2150